TRIPLE
Action

UNIT 3 BOOK

SCHOLASTIC INC.

Editor
Jeri Schapiro

Associate Editor
Julia Remine Piggin

Art Director
Carol Steinberg

Design
Sue Llewellyn

Production
Anna Ewing

Curriculum Consultants

Beverly Jones Ashbrook, Director of Reading,
Jefferson County Public Schools
Louisville, Kentucky

Joan Curry, Ed.D., Director of Clinical Training Center,
San Diego State University
San Diego, California

Charles Sherwood, Ed.D., Coordinator of Reading Education,
University of Mississippi
University, Mississippi

Illustrations and Photography: Jeanette Adams, pp. 127-136, 138; Abe Echevarria, p. 61; Warren Fricke, pp. 84-90, 143, 147-149, 151, 154; Robert Houser, pp. 49-54, 64-69, 72; Catherine Huerta, cover, pp. 35-40; Joel Naprstek, pp. 107, 110-113, 115, 116; Leo Pando, pp. 95, 98-101; Tim Raglin, pp. 5-9; Larry Ross, pp. 13-16, 18, 33, 44, 57, 59, 63, 76, 78, 79, 82, 97, 105, 109, 119, 120, 122, 123, 125, 145; Harvey Stein, pp. 21, 22, 24, 25, 27, 30; Culver Pictures, Inc., p. 30.

Grateful acknowledgment is made to the following authors and publishers for the use of copyrighted materials. Every effort has been made to obtain permission to use previously published material. Any errors or omissions are unintentional.

Scott Meredith Literary Agency, Inc., 845 Third Avenue, New York, NY 10022 for the adaptation of "Rebound" by Fredric Brown from NIGHTMARES AND GEEZENSTACKS, copyright © 1961 by Fredric Brown.

James McKimmey for the adaptation of his story, "The Eyes Have It," copyright © 1953 by James McKimmey.

Albert F. Nussbaum for the adaptation of his story, "The Dead Past," copyright © 1968 by H.S.D. Publications, Inc.

ISBN 0-590-30477-1

12 11

6 7 8 9/8 0 1/9

TABLE OF CONTENTS

VOCABULARY STUDY

canine   Inc.   jeweled   pedigree   pouted
hyena   intimidated   leash   piranha   sneakily

The new words belong in the "shaggy dog" story below. Write them above the underlined words that tell their meanings. The first one is done for you.

hyena
"I laugh a lot," said the night-time animal. "But I never cry."

"Neither do I," said the gorilla. He stuck out his lips, looking angry. "What makes you think I do?"

"Why should I cry?" said the man-eating fish from his tank.

"Why should I?" the French poodle chimed in. "I am a special dog with a paper telling who my parents were. Even this cord they lead me with is covered with valuable stones. Everything I have comes from Pampered Pets, Incorporated."

"Well, I'd cry with shame if I were scared by another animal," the lion said. "But, of course, that never happens."

Just then a little gray moth flew by. "How about you, little moth?" the lion asked. "Do you ever cry?"

"I cry," said the little gray moth. "Of course, I cry." Then, without warning, she said, "Haven't you ever seen a moth bawl?"

NEVER PROMISE YOUR SISTER A SNAKE

When you give your word, you shouldn't back down. A person can end up in the "dog house" for not keeping a promise....

NEVER PROMISE YOUR SISTER A SNAKE by Herb and Mary Montgomery

I'm the kind of person who does dumb things. My kid sister, Liz, is the kind of person who remembers dumb things.

The dumb thing I did was promise my sister a snake. Liz is five years old. She's always waiting at the door for me when I come home.

"Where's my snake?" she asks. "Did you bring me my snake, Jaime? Is it in your pocket?"

"No," I say, or, "I . . . I . . . ah . . . forgot."

Little sisters like mine do not take no for an answer. Liz cries, stamps her feet, and yells, "You promised, Jaime! You promised me a snake."

"It was a joke," I told her last night.

"A joke?" Liz pouted. Then she gazed into my eyes and said very sneakily, "You hate animals and tell lies."

"Hey, no way!" I complained. I knew I had said the wrong thing. She had me cornered.

Liz looked up at me and said, "Then you'll bring me a snake tomorrow?" It was more like an order than a question.

"Sure," I said, just wanting to get

rid of her. "Or maybe a dog..."

"A DOG!" Liz screamed. "Oh, Jaime, you're super. I love dogs! And I just l-o-v-e my b-i-g sister. Big sisters can do anything."

How do you say no forever to a little sister like that?

On my way home the next afternoon I stopped at a pet shop. The sign said: *Pets of the World, Inc*.

There was carpeting on the floor and perfume in the air. A man carrying a jeweled cigarette holder slipped up next to me. "May I help you in your search for an animal friend?" he asked.

"Sorry," I joked, "I've already got a boyfriend."

He gave me a stony stare. This was not a man with a sense of humor.

"Do...do you have any dogs?" I asked. "I'd like one for my little sister."

"No," he said.

"I beg your pardon?"

"We have no *ordinary* dogs!" he said again. "We have only pedigreed canines. Each of our lovely animals has papers."

"Well, how much for a plain one without the wrapping?" I asked, never one to be intimidated by fancy words.

"Two-fifty and up," the salesman said. He reached into a cage to pet a snake that was as big around as my arm.

I reached into my wallet, pulled out two dollars and fifty cents, and put it on the counter. "I'll take one of your dogs...ah...I mean canines," I said.

Just then a hyena laughed and an owl hooted.

"And how do you want to handle the balance?" the pet salesman asked.

"You mean for a leash, a food plate, and stuff like that?" I asked.

"I mean," he said, "the two hundred and forty-seven dollar and fifty-cent balance."

If I hadn't spent most of my weekly allowance, I would have walked out and left my two-fifty on the counter. But instead, I faked it and said, "Just kidding." I swept the money back into my hand. I wanted to get out of there fast, but in my hurry I dropped a quarter. It rolled into a cage. The animal there looked like the beady kind you see women wearing around their necks in old movies.

The animal sniffed the coin and pushed it out of the cage. He then dipped his paw in water and licked it clean. Big-time animals wanted nothing to do with my small-time change. I picked up the coin and shoved it into my pocket.

"Do you carry goldfish?" I asked, thinking about going home. I didn't want to face my little sister one more

time without some kind of pet.

"We don't stock them," the man said. "You'll have to check in a dime store. However, we have some lovely piranhas—"

"For a child?"

"They teach children respect," he said with a sly grin.

"No doubt about that," I agreed.

I made my retreat through *Pets of the World, Inc*. It seemed that every animal was looking down its nose at me. I felt like going home to get the

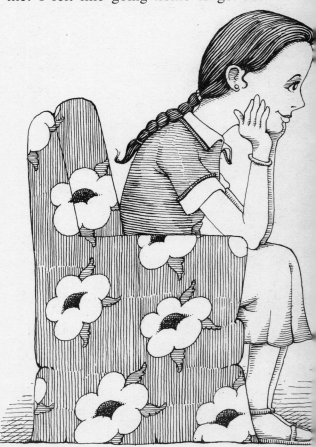

family photo album and show them *my* pedigree.

Where can you get a plain old dog these days? I worried. Liz was really going to put me down if I came home without a pet. *I have to find a mutt somewhere*, I told myself.

So I went to the city dog pound.

"You like dogs?" the woman in overalls barked over the sound of yipping and yapping.

"Love 'em," I said, trying to avoid an over-friendly German shepherd.

The place had a real honest dog-air — no perfume here.

When I got home with the dog, Liz cried, "You're the b-e-s-t, best sister in the whole world!"

So now we've gotten into pets at our house. The dog we have is one of a kind and Liz loves him. Of course, visitors sometimes ask if our dog has papers.

"Sure," Liz always says, "but Mommy makes me pick them up before we have company."

READING CHECK

Directions: When answers are given, put the letter for the right answer in the space. When answers are *not* given, write your answer in the space.

WORD MEANING FROM CONTEXT

1. In this story, the word *pound* means _____.
   a. to hit over and over
   b. 16 ounces
   c. a place for lost dogs

2. In this story, the word *retreat* means _____.
   a. a quiet place
   b. backing down and getting out
   c. a second ice cream cone

3. "And how do you want to handle the balance?" When the salesman said this, he meant: _____
   a. How are you going to arrange to pay for the amount still due?
   b. How will you know if you are getting a good buy?
   c. How will you manage to weigh the animals?

4. "Each of our lovely animals has papers." The salesman meant _____.
   a. they had records to prove their pedigree, or purity of breed
   b. they came with directions for house training
   c. they had paper clothing to keep them warm

MAIN IDEA/DETAILS

5. The pet shop was for people with money. Three reasons for thinking

   so are _____

   _____.

SEQUENCE

6. Jaime thought of buying her sister a goldfish after _____

_____.

FINDING PROOF

7. Jaime cared about Liz. Proof of this is _____

_____.

CAUSE AND EFFECT

8. Jaime left the pet shop and went to the dog pound because _____

_____.

MAKING INFERENCES

9. In the fancy pet shop, Jaime felt _____.

WHAT DO YOU THINK?

Do you think a promise should always be kept? Even if it's a dumb one? Do you think Jaime got out of it in a smart way?

How did the salesman make Jaime feel? When he said, "You'll have to check in a dime store," was he being helpful? Or was he trying to make Jaime feel cheap and small?

When the salesman said that piranhas — man-eating fish — would teach children respect, what did he mean? How do you think he felt about children?

Do you think Liz would have been happier with a dog with a pedigree? Would she have loved it more than the dog Jaime brought her?

WHAT DOES THE AUTHOR THINK?

When authors describe something or someone, they often let you know what they think about it. They do this by the words they choose. The same thing can be described in many ways, depending on what the author thinks. Here, for example, are two descriptions of the same dog.

The dog wasn't young, but he was trim. His deep red coat glowed like satin. His gentle brown eyes were filled with understanding.

The old mutt was thin, with a rusty, slippery-looking hide. He looked at us out of dull, mud-colored eyes as if to say, ''I know all about you.''

1. How does the author of the first paragraph feel about the dog?

_____

What are three words or phrases that give you the author's point of view? _____

_____

2. How does the author of the second paragraph feel about the dog?

_____

What are three words or phrases that give you the author's point of view? _____

_____

As you can see, some words paint a pleasant picture, and make you think the author had good feelings about the subject. Other words let you know that he or she didn't like the subject very much. Look back at the two descriptions. Which words show approval? Which words show disapproval?

Read the two descriptions that follow. Write the letter of the choice that best tells how the writer felt. Then write the four words or phrases that give you the feeling.

From the window of the train, the town looked bleak and cold. The buildings were all of rough, gray stone. The streets were dirty, with piles of snow and garbage at every corner. I saw only one person — a beggar dressed in rags, picking through the garbage.

The writer found the town ____.
a. unpleasant
b. pleasant
c. scary

Four words or phrases that suggest this feeling are: _____

_____

_____ .

The streetlights of the little town winked cheerfully. Clean white snow shone in the yellow light. An apple-cheeked girl danced in the street. She laughed as her dog bounced in and out of the drifts.

The writer ＿＿＿.
a. thought the town was not real
b. hated the look of the town
c. liked the look of the town

Four words or phrases that suggest this are: ＿＿＿＿＿＿＿＿

＿＿＿＿＿＿＿＿＿＿＿＿＿＿＿＿＿＿＿＿＿.

Think of a place you either like or dislike. It could be your town, your school, your room. Below, list some words and phrases you would use to describe that place. Try to choose words that show how you feel.

＿＿＿＿＿＿＿＿＿＿＿＿＿＿＿＿＿＿＿＿＿＿＿＿

＿＿＿＿＿＿＿＿＿＿＿＿＿＿＿＿＿＿＿＿＿＿＿＿

＿＿＿＿＿＿＿＿＿＿＿＿＿＿＿＿＿＿＿＿＿＿＿＿

＿＿＿＿＿＿＿＿＿＿＿＿＿＿＿＿＿＿＿＿＿＿＿＿

＿＿＿＿＿＿＿＿＿＿＿＿＿＿＿＿＿＿＿＿＿＿＿＿

Can you infer how authors feel about their characters? Read the paragraphs below. Then answer the questions that follow.

"I have never been drawn to members of the animal kingdom," said the General stiffly. He looked without interest at our dear pet, Towser. "Canines and other beasts do not belong in houses."

The author thinks the General is _____.
a. loving, but a little silly
b. warm and understanding
c. cold and a bit stuffy in his speech

Four words or phrases that suggest this are: _____

_____ .

Mrs. Moon's mouth turned down at the corners. "I'm old and poor," she whined, wiping a tear away with a lace handkerchief. "My fur coat is so out of style. There's just no use trying to go on when you're my age." Her voice was full of self-pity.

Mrs. Sherman's wrinkled face lit up with a smile. "I don't have much money," she laughed. "But who needs it at my age? I have a good warm coat and plenty to eat." She patted my hand. "I hope I live to be one hundred!"

The author _____.
a. likes Mrs. Moon and doesn't like Mrs. Sherman
b. likes Mrs. Sherman and doesn't like Mrs. Moon
c. feels the same about them both

Four words or phrases that suggest this are: _____

_____

_____

_____

Think of a TV, sports, or world personality you either like or dislike. Below, list some words and phrases you would use to describe that person. Try to choose words that show how you feel.

_____

_____

_____

_____

_____

_____

WHAT'S YOUR OPINION?

Does it make much difference whether you are the oldest or youngest child in your family? Whether you are an only child or one of many children? Here are some opinions. Pick one that you agree with. Then, in writing, give examples showing why you agree with it.

1. Being the oldest child isn't easy. It means taking care of younger brothers and sisters. It means doing more work around the house than they do. It means fighting for permission to do things that they won't have to fight for when they are older. By then, the parents won't be so worried about giving their children certain freedoms.

2. Oldest children are lucky. They are not bossed around by brothers and sisters. They often get a lot of attention from their parents. Parents may love all their children equally, but they may spend more time dealing with the problems of the first child. After all, a first child presents a whole new experience for them.

3. Being the youngest is tough. It means being teased and pushed around by the other kids in the family. It means wanting to grow up, but being treated like a baby. Some parents don't want their last child to grow up.

4. The youngest child has it easy. As the "baby of the family," he or she isn't punished as often as the older children. Sometimes the youngest child gets away with a lot.

5. The middle child is the one who has a hard time. Parents may worry about the oldest child's problems, and they may "baby" the youngest child. The middle child may not get as much attention.

6. Middle children have advantages that the oldest and youngest don't have. They can get advice and help from older brothers and sisters. They can feel grown up by giving advice and help to younger brothers and sisters. Their parents may not be as strict with them as they were with the oldest. And their parents may let them grow up faster than the youngest.

7. It's lonely being an only child. An only child doesn't have sisters and brothers to fool around with and talk seriously with. Also, some parents put pressure on an only child to succeed. Maybe if they had other children, they wouldn't worry so much about an only child.

8. An only child often gets a lot of attention from parents. Only children have other benefits too. They don't have to take care of younger brothers and sisters. They're not bossed around by older brothers and sisters. Their parents can spend more time and money on them than if there were other children too.

9. Generally, it doesn't make much difference whether you are the oldest, a middle, the youngest, or an only child. Happiness — or unhappiness — depends on other things.

Your Opinion: _____

_____

_____

_____ .

VOCABULARY STUDY

| amateur | clinching | disgusted | heavyweight | retired |
| champ | disgrace | foul | protest | tangled |

Words that have opposite meanings are called **antonyms.** Write the new words that are antonyms for the words below.

1. The opposite of *employed* is _____.

2. The opposite of *loser* is _____.

3. The opposite of *lightweight* is _____.

4. The opposite of *pleased* is _____.

5. The opposite of *pro* is _____.

6. The opposite of *honor* or *respect* is _____.

7. The opposite of *playing by the rules* is *to make a* _____.

8. The opposite of *approve* or *support* is _____.

9. The opposite of *neatly arranged* is _____.

10. In boxing, the opposite of *letting go* is _____.

POP'S BOY

Pop managed fighters, and he wanted a winner.
But he had more reasons than the winner knew.

POP'S BOY by Irvin Ashkenazy

The truck brought me as far as Lake City. I went into an all-night diner and ordered a hamburger.

The only other person there was an old man. He smiled when he saw the University of Florida sticker on my bag.

"Didn't I see you at the University one night last spring?" he asked. "You won the state amateur heavyweight title?"

I nodded.

"You didn't have those scars over your eyes then," he added.

I had turned pro, I told him.

"You quit school?" he asked.

"No," I said. "I turned pro to stay in school."

After a while, the old man got off his seat. "If you're going to the University," he said, "I can take you. I'm going that way."

As we drove, Pop told stories about the great fighters he had managed. He said he was "sort of retired." But he was looking for a heavyweight to fight Billy Terry. The fight was set for the next night. The man who was supposed to fight Terry had broken his hand in training.

By now it was almost morning. I told Pop I would hitch another ride.

"I thought you were going back to school," he said.

"I am. But first I have to pick up some money from a man named Willie," I said. "He was payoff man for a manager who took me on tour. I still have $500 coming to me. And I'm going to try to find that Willie."

"Forget about it," Pop said. "Charge it off to education."

"I won't get any more education," I said, "if I don't get that money. I need $300 to pay off last year's bills. Then I can get started on this year."

Pop was quiet for a while. Then he said, "Who did you fight this past summer?"

I named a few people. I told him how the manager had matched me in 10-round fights right from the start.

"That creep!" Pop said. "Throwing you in with guys like that! Did you stay the whole time with any of them?"

I took out some worn newspaper clippings. Pop almost went off the road, trying to read and drive at the same time.

"Well, I'll be..." he said. "You won them all!" After a few minutes he turned to me. "Stay over. I'll put you in against Billy Terry. You'll get your $300."

Later I met Pop's landlady. "Is he the one to fight Billy?" she asked Pop.

"He's my boy," Pop answered.

The landlady gave me something to eat. Then I went to Pop's room to get some sleep. When I woke up, a short man was looking down at me.

"This is J.D., my trainer," Pop explained.

While I got dressed, the three of us talked. I said I had heard of Terry a few years ago. I remembered that he had been pretty good. But I wondered what he had done since.

"He has disgraced the name he is fighting under," Pop said bitterly. "Tonight he's trying to make a comeback. He's going to try to win. No one is paying him to lie down this time!"

I asked Pop if Terry could still fight. Pop nodded slowly. "He could have been heavyweight champ. But he didn't listen to me."

I must have looked surprised. "I used to manage him," Pop added quickly.

When it was time to go to the fight, Pop put his arm around me. "This boy you're fighting is good," he said. "He can hit and he can box. But he does his training in dance halls. Hold him for six rounds and he's through. But until then — watch it! He's tricky and he's dirty."

I moved out at the sound of the bell. Terry came across the ring, fast. I stepped back and caught everything on arms, gloves, and shoulders. I let him come, moving in a circle. When he closed in, I tangled his arms without clinching.

Terry saw that I was no amateur. He was afraid. He needed to win badly. Suddenly, he put his thumb into my eye. I fell against the ropes, unable to see. Terry's punches kept coming at my head. Then he smashed me in the kidneys. I managed to fall into a clinch. Terry pulled out with a hard butt of his head on mine. Then the bell rang.

Pop protested the foul to the referee. But the referee only shrugged. He said he hadn't seen it.

During the second round, Terry rushed me. I pushed him from me with all my strength. He went right across the ring and into the ropes. He bounced off them as I came charging in.

Next thing I knew, I lay upon a cloud. I was floating in space. I heard

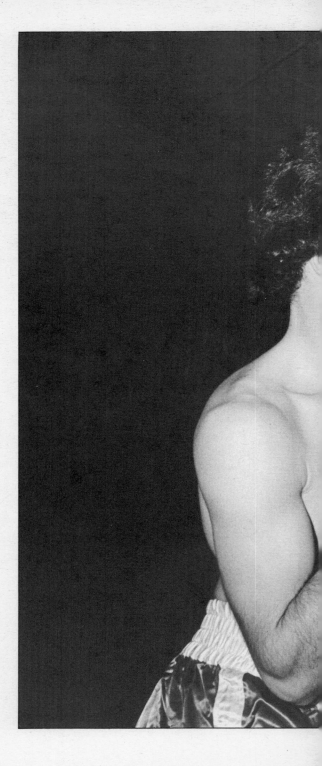

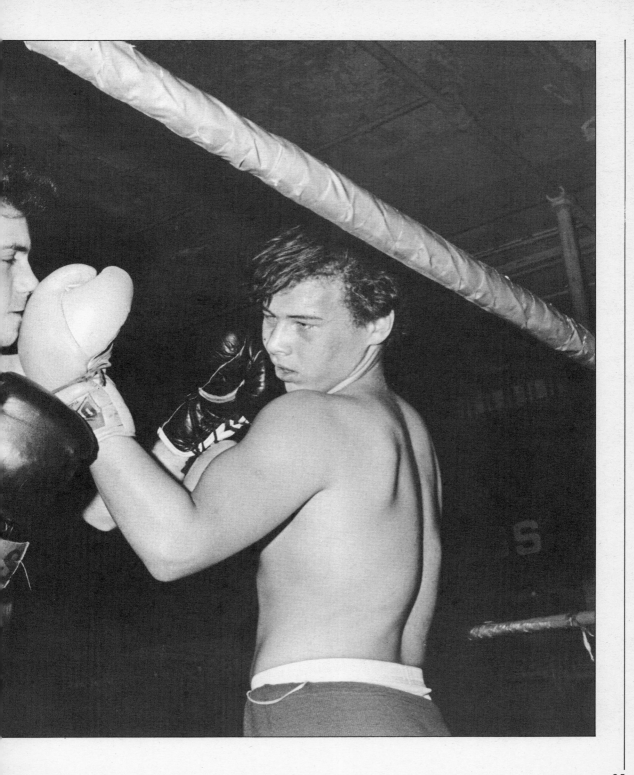

a far-off voice say, "Six! Seven!" At "Eight!" I got to one knee. And at "Nine!" I was on my feet.

Terry moved in fast now. He was trying for the finishing blow. But I stopped him. I turned so that his back was on the ropes. I let my full 170 pounds press against him. Then I dragged him along the ropes. I knew they were burning across his back. Moving in close, I stamped hard on his feet.

Then we were really at each other. We were both getting tired from throwing all those punches. Terry tried some dirty moves, but this time I was prepared. I hit him with the heel of my hand instead of the knuckles. I knew the glove laces would hurt him. As the referee came between us, I followed through with a hook. It smashed against Terry's jaw. He plunged to the floor.

I climbed through the ropes without waiting to hear the end of the count. I was disgusted by the whole match. Pop moved suddenly into the ring. He lifted Terry in his arms and dragged him to his corner.

I met Pop in a restaurant afterward. He looked very tired as he gave me a roll of bills. I counted $300. Then I handed him $75 of it.

"What's that for?" he asked.

I told him it was his cut. He pushed the money toward me. "You don't owe me nothing, son," he said.

I was quiet for a while. "I'm sorry I had to fight dirty," I finally said. "But you saw what he did."

Pop nodded. He wasn't looking at me. "You figure on graduating?" he said at last.

I told him I guessed so. I was a bit surprised that he had asked.

"Finish school," he told me. "Make something of yourself."

Just then, J.D. hurried in. "We'll just about make the bus," he told Pop. "Aren't you coming to the station with us?"

Pop just sat there. "To tell you the truth," he said, "I'm kind of beat."

I grabbed his hand as I left. "So long, Pop...and thanks for everything."

J.D. saw me off at the bus station. "Pop will line up more easy money for you pretty soon," he told me.

"Tonight's money was not easy," I told him. "But it was the fastest $300 I've ever made."

J.D.'s eyes grew small. "You don't have to fool me, kid. I saw the manager give Pop the $130 for your pay."

The bus started up before I could answer. But the next day I wrote Pop. I figured he must have taken the rest of the money out of his own pocket. I wanted to ask him about it. I didn't know his address, so I sent the letter to to the ring. I wrote him two more times. But my letters came back. They were marked "Not here."

Two months later, I got a wire from J.D. He had a fight for me in Tampa. He met me at the station.

"How's Pop?" I asked the moment I saw him.

J.D. stopped short. "Didn't you know? Pop's dead."

I felt as though someone had kicked me in the stomach. "When did it happen?" I asked weakly.

"The next morning after you left," J.D. told me, "his landlady found him in bed — dead." He tapped his chest and said, "He just gave out."

It was a minute or two before I could speak again. "Did Pop have any family?"

"Just that one kid," J.D. said.

"What kid?"

J.D. looked at me. Then a funny look came over his face. "Didn't you know? Billy Terry was Pop's son."

READING CHECK

WORD MEANING FROM CONTEXT

1. Terry was a "dirty fighter." This means that ____.
   a. he never took a bath
   b. he did not fight by the rules
   c. he rubbed his gloves in dirt before a fight

2. "Two months later, I got a wire from J.D." The word *wire* means ____.
   a. a thin thread of metal
   b. a telegram
   c. material for a fence

MAIN IDEA

3. Another title for this story might be _____.

DETAILS

4. The fact that Billy Terry is Pop's son comes as a surprise at the end of the story. Reread the story and find two details that are clues to this fact. _____

_____

SEQUENCE

5. The narrator fought several 10-round matches ____.
   a. before he met Pop
   b. after he met Pop
   c. after Pop died

FINDING PROOF

6. Pop was disappointed in Billy Terry. Proof of this is _____

_____.

CAUSE AND EFFECT

7. Billy Terry probably fought dirty because _____

_____.

MAKING INFERENCES

8. Why did Pop make sure the narrator got $300 for the fight? _____

_____

WHAT DO YOU THINK?

Compare Pop's feelings toward Billy Terry with his feelings toward
the narrator. Do you think Pop wanted his son to be beaten in the ring?
If so, why? Was it for his own good, or just because Pop was ashamed
of him? Did Pop really love Terry? If you think so, why? Was what
happened in the ring a cause of Pop's death?

How do you think the narrator felt at the end of the story?

WHAT'S THE MEANING?

Almost anything can be said in more than one way. Here are some things that were said in the story "Pop's Boy." After them is a list of statements that mean the same. Write the letter of each statement next to the one it matches.

_____ "I followed through with a hook."

_____ "Charge it off to education."

_____ "Make something of yourself."

_____ "I'm kind of beat."

_____ "He does his training in dance halls."

_____ "No one is paying him to lie down this time."

a. Instead of working out, he stays up all night having a good time.

b. I'm worn out and tired.

c. So, you lost, but it taught you something.

d. I bent my elbow, kept it stiff, and hit him again.

e. Don't be a bum — study and get ahead in the world.

f. Last time he let himself get knocked out for money. This time, nobody offered him money to throw the fight.

Here are some other sentences, followed by another list. Match them up in the same way.

_____ It's gone with the wind.

_____ He ate until I thought he'd burst.

_____ If you want a thing well done, do it yourself.

_____ She tried to feed me a lot of soft soap.

_____ That's like yelling "Fire!" in a crowded theater.

_____ I looked at the gun and knew it was time for me to say my prayers.

_____ If it had been a bear, it would have bitten you.

_____ Right now she doesn't even know her own name.

_____ I told him to put up or shut up.

_____ I don't buy that.

a. So much is happening that she's all mixed up.

b. It was so close to you, I don't see how you missed it.

c. Sometimes, help is more trouble than it's worth.

d. You're scaring people so they may act foolishly.

e. I don't believe it.

f. It's all over, forever.

g. He made a pig of himself.

h. She told me a lot of nice things I knew she didn't mean.

i. I was afraid I'd be killed.

j. He should either prove what he's saying, or stop talking about it.

Below are eight sentences. Then there are three sentences under each. Check the sentence that says the same things as the boldface sentence. Watch out — they're tricky!

1. **The man wore a wrinkled old suit.**

_____ a. The suit the old man wore was wrinkled.

_____ b. The wrinkled man wore an old suit.

_____ c. The suit the man wore was old and wrinkled.

2. **The chef made Ray a salad.**

_____ a. Ray made a chef salad.

_____ b. The chef made a salad for Ray.

_____ c. Ray's salad was for the chef.

3. **The man who had been drinking was fined by the judge.**

_____ a. The man was fined by the judge who had been drinking.

_____ b. The judge gave a fine to the man who had been drinking.

_____ c. The man was fine, but the judge had been drinking.

4. **The young woman outside owns a small car.**

_____ a. The small car that is outside belongs to the young woman.

_____ b. The young woman who is outside owns a small car.

_____ c. The young woman's car is outside.

5. **When John was five, his father died and left three children.**

_____ a. John's father died at age five, leaving three children.

_____ b. John's father died and left three children when John was five.

_____ c. When he died, John's father left his children to John.

6. **The thief was captured by the police before anything was stolen.**

_____ a. Before the thief was captured, he stole everything.

_____ b. The thief was captured before anything was stolen by the police.

_____ c. Before anything was stolen, the police captured the thief.

7. **The vase that was bought by the woman was slightly cracked.**

_____ a. The woman who bought the vase was slightly cracked.

_____ b. The vase the woman bought was slightly cracked.

_____ c. The woman cracked the vase and had to buy it.

8. **Either Bert or Harry won the prize.**

_____ a. Neither Bert nor Harry won the prize.

_____ b. One of the two men, Bert or Harry, won the prize.

_____ c. Both Bert and Harry won the prize.

VOCABULARY STUDY

accompanied — go with
choir — group of singers
conquered — won over
disturb — bother
ditties — songs
draped — covered
emergency — sudden trouble
enforcement — making sure something is working

fateful — important to the future
intent — plan
obvious — very clear
plunge — an important step
romantic — as if in a dream or story
rumor — something said but not proved
sheriff — law officer

In the following paragraph, the names of musical instruments have been used in place of words from the list above. Cross out the name of the musical instrument, and write in the word that makes sense in the sentence. The first one is done for you.

My sister made a ~~kazoo~~ *fateful* yet wise decision. She is going to take the harmonica and marry the violin, the man who wears the silver star in our town. At first, we thought it was only a trombone, but now her guitar is clear.

It is also kazoo that law harmonica is not on her future husband's mind since he tromboned her heart. Not even the biggest violin would kazoo his calm. He walks around with a guitar look on his face all the time. It's as if he's listening to a piano singing love trombones, guitared by smiling angels violined in flowing white robes.

THE BATTLE OF IDA

Music is supposed to make people happy. Music is a good thing. But like any good thing, sometimes you can get too much of it.

THE BATTLE OF IDA by Carol Ellis

Until last summer, nobody in Ida thought much about the old iron cannon in the park. I'm not sure anyone even knew what it was used for. There's no "Battle of Ida" anywhere in the history books, and we just used it for fun. Little kids climbed on it and big kids decorated it with toilet paper. (I've done both in my time.) But then something happened, and now Ida's cannon has a history that everybody knows.

If you're thinking that Ida is a small town, you're right. These days *less* is supposed to be *more*, so Ida is proud to be small. ("Welcome to Ida, the Tiny Town with the Big Heart! Pop. 4702.") But when you get to be 15 or 16, *less* can also be boring. There's just not much to do, especially in the summer. Covering the cannon with toilet paper is good for only so many laughs. That's the main reason Josie, Louis, and I did what we did. We were bored. Another reason was, we wanted to make some money.

"Street musicians? In Ida? You're crazy, Andy!" (It takes Josie a while to see the value of a good idea.)

"Wait a minute, Josie. Let's hear him out." (Louis likes to know exactly what he's getting into before he makes a move.)

"It's simple." (It was my idea — I

felt responsible for it.) "We're going to bring music to the streets of Ida and we're going to make money doing it. We can't miss because Ida has never seen anything like it. It's different, it's romantic, it's—"

"A good way to meet girls." (Louis was coming around.)

"OK. But we can't just wander the streets. We have to be organized." (Once Josie started improving on an idea, I knew I had her.) "Sure! We hit different places at different times — whenever there's a crowd."

Ida *does* have crowds once in a while — moviegoers, picnickers in the park, shoppers on Main Street. So on Friday morning, armed with a harmonica (me), a guitar (Josie), and bongos (Louis), we stationed ourselves at the corner of Main and Marigold. At first we didn't draw a crowd. We drew Hacksetter.

C.T. Hacksetter is Ida's Chief Law Enforcement Officer. (There are only three.) No one calls him Chief or Sheriff, though. We just call him Hacksetter. He's basically a nice guy — he just likes to put on his Chief Law Enforcement Officer Act.

"OK, what's going on here?" (Hacksetter is slightly deaf, so he tends to shout.)

"Nothing, Hacksetter. We're just making a little music, that's all." (I thought it was obvious.)

"I can hear *that*, Andy. I've got ears! What I want to know is why you're standing here playing folk ditties when people are trying to shop."

"Well, Hacksetter, that's the point." (Louis is big on being reasonable.) "We thought we'd have a better chance of making money if we played where the people are."

(I decided to plunge in again.) "That's right. We're street musicians. A lot of places have them — New York, San Francisco...."

"Yeah. There's no law against it, is there?" (We didn't know it then, but Josie had spoken fateful words.)

"Nope. No law at all. But don't let me catch you disturbing the peace or blocking traffic."

"Don't worry," we said.

"So? Go ahead! Make music!"

While Hacksetter was shouting at us, a crowd had formed. We played — and they stayed. Then — they *paid*! And they kept staying and paying all day, wherever we went. The people loved us and proved it with money — not just nickels and dimes, either. Plenty of dollar bills floated into the open guitar case. We were a hit. We'd conquered the town of Ida! And like all conquerers, we patted ourselves on the backs and bragged about it. That was our first mistake.

"Andy! Did you hear? Did you

hear?" (When Josie is upset, she repeats herself.)

"Hear what? Come on, we've got to meet Louis in the park."

"But that's just it! There's another group...there's another group of musicians in the park!"

Josie was wrong. There were *two* groups of musicians in the park. There was another one at the movies and three more on Main Street. All the kids we'd bragged to had dusted off their banjos, violins, and kazoos. Now they were imitating us!

"Hey!" Mrs. Jackson was screaming from her upstairs window. "Do you mind? I'm trying to hear the ballgame!"

"Sorry, Mrs. Jackson. But we have a right to be here. There's no law against it."

"OK! OK! Just wait!" We waited long enough for Mrs. Jackson to drag her TV to the window and blast us with sounds of the Red Sox beating the Yankees. Then we moved on.

But it was the same wherever we went. All over town, the people of Ida were fighting back against the street musicians. And they were doing it with sound. Loudspeakers appeared in windows. Radios and televisions were turned up full volume. Choir practice was held on the lawns. (I heard a rumor that Mr. Ingram dragged his upright piano onto the sidewalk and played marching songs, accompanied by his trombone-tooting niece.) By Saturday evening, Ida was full of sound and fury. That's when it happened.

Josie, Louis, and I were trying to find sidewalk space on Main Street when we heard a tremendous explosion. Then—silence.

"I don't believe it!" Louis said, getting excited. "That was the old cannon in the park!"

In a second, everybody was running toward Ida Park. We arrived just as

"OK, OK. Everything's cool." (Louis was calm, as usual.) "There's plenty of room for everybody, right?"

Wrong. There isn't plenty of room for a lot of street musicians in Ida, because there aren't a lot of streets in Ida. But nobody cared about that. Pride was at stake. By Saturday afternoon we were all battling for territory, using music as a weapon. We forgot Hacksetter's warning about disturbing the peace. Since there were so many of us, we disturbed a lot of peace. That was our second mistake.

Hacksetter did.

"All right! Who shot the cannon?"

"The correct word is 'fire,' Hacksetter," Mrs. Cunningham explained, dusting off her hands. "And we did it — my husband and I."

"That's right," Mr. Cunningham said, patting the cannon. "I know you don't hear too well, Hacksetter, so maybe you missed all the music and noise today. But Mrs. C. and I couldn't take it anymore. We don't have a TV, we don't play any instruments, and our radio's busted. So, we fired the cannon."

"I've got ears, Cunningham!" (Hacksetter's face was getting all puffed out.) "I heard the noise. What do you think I've been doing all day?"

"I don't know, Hacksetter. But you didn't stop all the noise." Mr. Cunningham patted the cannon again. "*We* did that!"

He was right. Ida was completely silent. And it stayed that way, because after Hacksetter calmed down, he read the results of the emergency town-council meeting. (That's where he'd been all afternoon.) It banned people "with intent to make music and money" from the streets of Ida until further notice.

But like Mr. Cunningham said, Hacksetter didn't stop the "Battle of Ida." The old cannon did. And that's how it got its new history. It's still draped with kids by day and toilet paper by night. But now there's a sign on it too: "The Cannon of Ida. Fired for Peace, June, 1978. No Noise Is Good Noise."

READING CHECK

WORD MEANING FROM CONTEXT

1. "By Saturday evening, Ida was full of sound and fury." The word *fury* means ____.
   a. humor
   b. anger
   c. animal hairs

2. "...we patted ourselves on the backs and bragged about it." The word *brag* means ____.
   a. to cry
   b. to worry
   c. to boast or show off

3. "...we were all battling for territory, using music as a weapon." This means that ____.
   a. groups of musicians were competing with each other for the town's attention
   b. fights broke out between the musicians
   c. the musicians ran the townspeople out of town

MAIN IDEA/DETAILS

4. Having street musicians was a good idea until it got out of hand.

Find two examples from the story to support this statement. _____

_____

_____

_____ .

SEQUENCE

5. The town council decided to ban street musicians after _____

_____.

CAUSE AND EFFECT

6. Someone fired the cannon because _____.

FINDING PROOF

7. The town of Ida was small. Proof is that _____

_____.

MAKING INFERENCES

8. After the "Battle of Ida" the people felt differently about their town
and each other. How? _____

_____.

WHAT DO YOU THINK?

Do you think forming street music groups was a good idea? Have you done anything like that because you were bored? At first, the townspeople seemed to enjoy the music. What proof is there in the story? When did their attitude change? For what reason? Should the street musicians have stopped playing when people complained? Was the law the council passed a fair one?

CONNECTIVES

**"We thought we'd have a better chance making money.
We played where the people are."**

**"There isn't plenty of room for a lot of street musicians in Ida.
There aren't a lot of streets in Ida."**

The sentences above are from the story "The Battle of Ida." They make sense, but they sound odd. One idea doesn't flow into the other. Why? Because something is missing — some words called "connectives."

Connectives are like bridges over rivers. They connect one thought with another so a journey through a story will be smooth. Connectives help make the author's meaning clear.

The connecting word missing in the first example is **if**: "We thought we'd have a better chance of making money IF we played where the people are." In the second example, the connecting word is **because**: "There isn't plenty of room for a lot of street musicians in Ida BECAUSE there aren't a lot of streets in Ida."

These are only two of the many connectives that help out in reading and writing. Here are some others:

when	**unless**	**so**	**if**
first	**before**	**or**	**until**
but	**second**	**while**	**because**

The sentences that follow are each missing a **connective**. Find the word in the list that best connects the two parts of the sentence. Write it in the space. Use each word just once.

1. George wanted to go to the game, _____ his father wouldn't let him.

2. "You can't go, George, _____ you've taken the fish out of the tank again."

3. "But, Dad, the fish looked unhappy in the tank, _____ I set them free."

4. "Did you drop them in the river, _____ did you take them to the lake?"

5. "I had several ideas: _____, I thought of putting them in the river; _____, I thought of taking them to the public aquarium...."

6. "George, you won't leave this house, _____ you say what you did with the fish!"

7. "I'll tell you, Dad, _____ you promise not to get mad at me."

8. "I'm not promising anything _____ I hear the truth, George!"

9. "Well, Dad, I put them in the bathtub _____ you were out."

10. "Your mother will be very angry with you _____ she gets home from work."

11. "But, Dad, I cleaned the tub _____ I put the fish in."

In each sentence below, you will find two "joining" words in parentheses. Choose the word that makes sense, and underline it.

1. Do you know (**when, where**) this train is supposed to leave the station?

2. Ralph didn't know the answer (**unless, until**) Norma whispered it to him.

3. Brad isn't sure (**if, whether**) or not he will go with us tonight.

4. He's not sure yet, (**before, because**) he has a sore throat.

5. I'm not going bowling (**if, unless**) I feel better.

6. Roy didn't like his hair long, (**but, so**) he cut it.

7. Keith fell downstairs, (**and, but**) he didn't hurt himself.

8. (**Whether, If**) you're really my friend, you'll help me.

Look at the five pairs of sentences below. In each case, the first sentence is the same. But the second sentence of each pair is different. As you read them, notice the word or words in boldface.

1. Sheila played better than we had expected her to. **However**, the rest of the team played badly.
2. Sheila played better than we had expected her to. **Because of this**, the crowd gave her a standing ovation.
3. Sheila played better than we had expected her to. **For instance**, she did not miss a single foul shot.
4. Sheila played better than we had expected her to. **In addition**, she showed the most thoughtfulness for the players on the other team.
5. Sheila played better than we had expected her to. **Later**, she was given the Most Valuable Player award.

Look again at the boldface words. These connecting words are *signals* that tell a reader what to expect.

Some words signal that a writer will make a *contrast* with what he or she has just written. For example: **however, even so, but, on the other hand, at the same time, yet.**

Some words tell a reader that more information will be added. Here are some examples: **for example, for instance, in fact, in other words, also, and, in addition, besides, moreover.**

Some words tell a reader that a writer is about to finish what he or she has been saying. Here are some examples: **finally, therefore, at last, because of this, eventually.**

There are dozens of connecting words that writers use. Each has a certain meaning. The meaning shows how sentences and paragraphs are related.

Here are four pairs of sentences. In each case, the second sentence could begin with a connecting word. Think of a word or group of words that could introduce each second sentence, and write it in the space. Do not use *and, but,* or *or* in these sentences.

1. There are a lot of things I didn't like about that movie.

   _____, the acting was terrible.

2. He started collecting bottle caps in second grade.

   _____, his closet was full of them.

3. The rain showed no sign of letting up. _____, the picnic was ruined.

4. She wants to be a forest ranger because the pay is good.

   _____ she likes being outdoors.

The sentences below are followed by connecting words. Think of second sentences that could be introduced by the words given. Complete the second sentences on the line.

1. There are plenty of things I could do for a living. For instance,

   _____.

2. He just kept asking me over and over. Eventually, _____

   _____.

3. It would probably be interesting to climb that mountain. On the other

   hand, _____.

4. I didn't watch that show because it was on too late. Besides,

   _____.

VOCABULARY STUDY

| challenge | incredible | pose | somersault | thrust |
| hooted | jeering | sauntered | threatening | vanished |

Below is a "shaggy dog" story. Its ending has something to do with the next story you will read. As you read this way-out tale, unscramble the letters to write the correct word in each space.

The odd-looking stranger _____ (**netrausde**) into the Last Chance Café. He tried to look tough. At the bar, someone _____ (**deotoh**) like an owl.

The stranger _____ (**hustrt**) his hands into his pockets. "Laughing and _____ (**reenijg**) at me is a mistake," he said.

"Are you trying to _____ (**lengachel**) us to a fight?" Red Hawkins asked.

"No I'm not _____ (**eatennighrt**) anybody," the stranger said.

"Then your 'cool' is just a phony _____ (**sope**)."

"If I have made you angry," the stranger said, "I am sorry." And he jumped very high, turned a _____ (**mersoaustl**), and _____ (**ishnavde**) into thin air.

"That's _____ (**crediibeln**)!" said Red. "He's gone."

"Yes," said One-Tooth Hobbs. "He really jumped to conclusions!"

NEW KID IN TOWN

It's not easy being the new kid in town. People are quick to size you up. But then, some people are in for surprises.

NEW KID IN TOWN **by Karin Ireland**

Pete frowned and looked up uneasily at the three guys closing in on him. He never really minded being small, except that it made people jump to conclusions. Before a word was said, Pete picked out the leader. He was the one in the middle. And he was huge.

"Well, what do you say, Shorty?" asked the big guy. He thrust his hip forward in what he must have thought was a threatening pose.

Pete did feel a little threatened. Not that he couldn't handle the guy if he had to, but. . . .

"Since you're new," the big one drawled, "I'm going to let you buy me a Coke." He smiled a cool smile. It was the kind that spreads lips over teeth, but leaves the rest of the face untouched.

Pete stood for a moment, considering his choices. Finally, he shrugged his shoulders and dug into his jeans for a coin. The other boys moved to let him by, and he walked self-consciously to the soda machine.

The can clunked, and Pete walked back to the jeering group. He tried to act casual as he handed over the cold can. But he was mad and his body was all set to deck the guy.

"I'm Jack," the leader said, reach-

ing for the can. It was a challenge. "Who are you?"

Pete stood a moment before answering. "Pete Brown," he finally said.

"Brown, huh?" It was Jack, of course. His friends didn't seem to talk. "Is your old man that Brown guy on TV?"

"No, my dad came here to open a school. He teaches —"

"His own school," Jack repeated, cutting Pete off. "Listen, guys, you hear that?"

The group smiled and nodded, but remained speechless. Pete clamped his jaw shut and glared at Jack.

Just then the bell rang for the next class. Jack tipped his Coke to Pete and sauntered off with his friends close behind. Pete sighed and shook his head.

At lunch Pete ate with Tom, his only friend so far. "Just don't make him mad," Tom said when he heard about Jack. "He likes being the tough guy, and he does have an incredible right hook."

"Does he get to do whatever he wants?" asked Pete.

"Yes."

"Doesn't anybody stand up to him?"

"No. Nobody."

Pete changed the subject and they talked until Tom had to leave. Pete stayed, finishing his lunch. *Too bad*

Kim had the other lunch period, he thought. He wondered how she was doing.

Pete felt someone approaching and looked up. Jack and his friends flopped into the empty seats at the table. Pete's smile vanished. He took a bite of his hamburger and tried to ignore them.

"Hey," said Jack. "I need a date for Friday and I hear you have a sister." His laugh suggested trouble.

Pete continued to chew for a moment longer. Then he looked straight at Jack and said, "She's not my sister. Kim just came from Korea and is staying with us. You leave her alone. I mean it....."

"Well, excuse me!" Jack hooted. He turned to his audience. "Doesn't sound very friendly, does he? He must be having a bad day." Jack swiped Pete's carton of milk and swaggered toward the door. His friends followed after him faithfully.

When school was over, Pete went to find Kim. She was waiting at the spot they had arranged to meet. But Pete didn't like what he saw when he got there. Jack and his friends were standing around her, blocking her way.

Kim looked mad. Other kids who were passing laughed and joked. They didn't seem to notice what was going on.

Pete took a slow, deep breath. Then he walked over to the group. "Kim, are you ready?" he asked, ignoring the others. She flashed him a grateful smile.

"Beat it, Shorty," said Jack. "We're busy. Go find somebody else to talk to."

"Kim?" Pete repeated.

"I'm ready," she said. But no one moved to let her pass.

Pete reached across to take her hand. Suddenly, Jack turned and swung his right fist at Pete's jaw.

Pete stepped to the left, outside the punch. With his right hand, he blocked the blow. Then he turned an inside half-turn and grabbed Jack's fist. Pete gave a quick jerk and tossed Jack into a clumsy somersault.

Jack's friend's stood staring, with their mouths open. Jack sat on the floor, rubbing his arm and looking bewildered.

"You didn't let me finish before," Pete said. "My dad came here to open a school. He teaches people Judo and Karate."

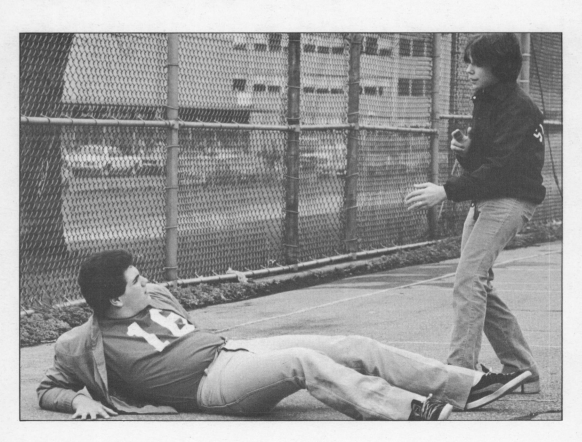

READING CHECK

WORD MEANING FROM CONTEXT

1. "Jack swiped Pete's carton of milk and swaggered to the door." The word *swaggered* means ____.
   a. ran
   b. walked confidently
   c. skipped

MAIN IDEA

2. The saying that best expresses the main idea of the story is: ____
   a. Nice guys finish last.
   b. Don't judge a book by its cover.
   c. Boys will be boys.

DETAILS

3. Pete's father had moved to town to _____
   _____.

SEQUENCE

4. Pete tossed Jack down to the ground after ____.
   a. Jack told Pete to buy him a Coke
   b. Jack stole Pete's milk
   c. Jack bothered Kim

FINDING PROOF

5. Pete could have beaten Jack any time. Proof of that is _____

_____ .

CAUSE AND EFFECT

6. At first Jack wasn't afraid of Pete because _____

_____ .

MAKING INFERENCES

7. Why do you think Pete waited so long to prove he could beat Jack?

_____

_____

WHAT DO YOU THINK?

What type of person was Jack? Do you know anybody like him? Why do you think nobody had ever stood up to him? How did Pete manage to flip Jack to the ground? What was Jack's reaction? Do you think he will treat Pete differently from now on?

FORESHADOWING

Sometimes authors give readers hints or clues that suggest what may happen later in a story. These hints or clues are called **foreshadowing**.

Think back to the story "New Kid in Town." As you read the story, did you have the feeling that Pete could take care of himself? Did you know, even before the end, that Jack was headed for trouble? You probably did. That's because the author used some foreshadowing hints to help build suspense, without quite giving away the ending.

Here is an example:

> **He never really minded being small, except it made people jump to conclusions.**

Look back over the story. What other examples can you find?

The story starters that follow contain **foreshadowing**. Read them, and then answer the questions.

There was a terrible storm the night before my cousin came to visit us. It kept me up all night. Trees split in two, and bricks from the chimney fell on the roof. "I think lightning struck the old tower," my father said.

But the next day was bright and sunny. My cousin and I walked across the wet green grass to the old tower. That's where we always went for our private talks. When we got there, we saw stones we had never seen before. They were lying at the base of the tower. *Where did the stones come from?* we wondered.

We went in and sat down on the damp ground. Light seemed to be streaming down from some new window. Suddenly, we heard a scraping sound. Dust powdered my cousin's hair.

1. What ideas in the story foreshadow or suggest that something unusual is about to happen? Underline the parts that give clues to what may happen next.

2. Using the foreshadowing clues, decide which of the sentences below describes what will probably happen. _____
   a. The storm starts up again. The cousins get wet, then very sick.
   b. The tower, weakened by the storm, falls in on the cousins and traps them inside.
   c. The cousins sit and talk for a while, then go out into the sunlight.

R-R-R-ING
R-R-R-ING

Tom jumped out of bed. "That dumb alarm clock!" he said to himself when he realized he had overslept. He decided to skip breakfast and dress in a hurry. First, he broke the laces of his sneakers. Next, two buttons popped off his shirt. He missed the school bus anyway, and had to walk to school. *Things couldn't get worse,* he figured. Or so he thought.

At school, Ms. Linkhart sprang a surprise quiz, and Tom got the lowest mark. *What next*? he wondered, on the way to the lunchroom. He spotted Carol at a table and went to join her. That's when he tripped and spilled his soup.

When he started to sit down, Carol looked at him coldly. "Tom," she began. Tom's heart sank.

1. What clues get you ready for something even worse ahead? Underline them.

2. Using the foreshadowing clues, which of the sentences below seems most likely to describe what Carol says to Tom? ____
   a. "Tom, about the dance you asked me to — the answer is yes. I'd love to go."
   b. "Oh, you've spilled your soup. Let me get you another cup."
   c. "Tom, I'm saving that seat for Paul. And by the way, he's taking me to the dance."

3. Based on what you've read, what might Tom be thinking? ____
   a. I wish I had stayed in bed.
   b. I don't like Carol anymore.
   c. This soup is terrible.

REBOUND by Fredric Brown

Here's a mini-story for you to enjoy. Its title foreshadows or gives a clue to the story's end. After you read the first paragraph, predict what you think will happen. Then read the story. You may be in for a surprise!

The Power came to Larry Snell suddenly — out of nowhere. How and why it came, he never learned.

It could have happened to a nicer guy. Snell was a small-time thief. His only good quality was cowardice. This kept him from committing murder.

The night it happened, he was talking to a bookie on the phone. He was arguing about a bet he had made. Finally, giving up, he said, "Drop dead," and hung up.

He thought nothing of it until the next day. He learned that the bookie *had* dropped dead, while talking on the phone. It had happened at the time of their conversation.

Was this more than a coincidence? Larry Snell wanted to find out. He made a list of 20 people he hated. He phoned them one at a time. He told each one to drop dead. They did — all of them.

It was not until the end of that week that he found he *really* had the Power. He was talking to another crook. He asked the crook how much money he had with him. Then, kidding, Snell said to hand it over. The crook did. It was almost $500.

By the end of the week, Snell was rich. He had demanded money from everyone he knew. He moved into a fancy hotel. He bought expensive clothes. He took women to restaurants and nightclubs.

It was a nice life. But after a while, Snell felt he was wasting the Power. Why shouldn't he use it to take over the world? He could become the most powerful dictator in history.

Since his commands were obeyed over the phone, he was sure they would be obeyed over television. All he had to demand was a world-wide TV broadcast. Then he would be heard by everyone everywhere.

This would be a big deal. He wanted to plan it carefully. He decided to spend several days alone to plan it all out.

He went to a hotel in the Catskill Mountains. He started taking long walks alone, planning and dreaming. He found a favorite spot. It was a small hill surrounded by mountains. He did most of his planning there. And he became more and more excited as he began to see that his plan could work.

He would become Emperor of the

World. Why not? Who could disobey a man with the Power? He had the Power to make anyone obey any command, including....

"Drop dead!" he shouted in his excitement.

Two teenagers found him there the next day. They hurried back to the village to report to the police. They had found a dead man on top of Echo Hill.

WHAT DO YOU THINK?

Did the story's end surprise you? What was Larry Snell's plan? How did it backfire?

VOCABULARY STUDY

choked	shrieked
disco	snicker
imitate	squealed
permission	stumbled
scowled	terrified

Below are some silly verses. The lines will rhyme if you put the words from above in place of the words that are underlined. Write the words that make the rhymes on the lines.

1. Go to the sink and put that dish in!
   To clean up the house you don't need an OK. _____

2. I won't go to the cave — there's a monster inside.
   The thought makes me shake, and I'm scared
   to death. _____

3. Outside, the lonely wolf howled,
   While inside, Aunt Millie looked angry. _____

4. I know it's funny, but you'll finish quicker
   If you tell yourself you're not going to laugh
   to yourself. _____

5. We got together and clowned and joked
   We laughed so much we almost couldn't
   breathe. _____

6. Polly got the apple peeled —
   A worm came out and Polly said "eek." _____

7. Learn to dance — don't wait,
   Just look around and copy what you see. _____

8. The wind blew, the old door squeaked,
   Something went "Whoooo!" and my sister
   gave a sharp scream. _____

9. Down the road the big truck rumbled,
   Crossing in front of it, Lucy tripped. _____

10. "Driving on the ice is an awful risk, Joe."
    "I know, but I've got to get to the place
    where people dance to records." _____

SHALL WE DANCE?

Some people don't fit in. Sometimes it's because they're not "as good as" other people. And sometimes, it's because they're better.

SHALL WE DANCE? by Stuart James

I guess you'd have to say that Olive Tease was a drip. She wasn't anybody you'd look at twice — well, not for the usual reasons. She wasn't bad-looking, really. But she dressed kind of funny. She lived with two old aunts, and I guess she got their old dresses. She wore black-rimmed glasses. Her hair was always pulled back in braids. She was like somebody out of another time.

Unless we got to talking about weird names, most of the kids didn't pay much attention to Olive Tease.

That is, until the day Johnny Miller asked her to dance.

Ms. Mansfield had gotten permission to turn one of the study halls into a disco during the lunch hour. She figured it would keep the kids from roaming the halls, since we weren't allowed to leave the building. There wasn't really anywhere else to go, so there was always a good crowd.

This one day the kids were milling around in little groups. A bunch of girls were doing a line dance. The big shots were gathered around Johnny

Miller as usual. Johnny was something else. He never had to work at being the best football player, the best student, the best dancer. It all just came naturally to him. He drew people to him like a magnet. He was the most popular kid in the school.

Johnny was standing against the wall, smiling, as his eyes swept the room. Suddenly, he left his little clique and started across the floor.

Every girl in the room looked to see where he was going. He was heading straight for Olive Tease. She was sitting alone against the wall. The seats on either side of her were vacant. As Johnny approached, Olive glanced right and left at the empty seats. It looked as though she hoped to find some pretty girl sitting there. She looked absolutely terrified.

Johnny stopped in front of her, smiled, and held out both hands. When she didn't move, he said, "Please?" Her hands rose from her lap, slowly. Johnny took both her hands — still smiling — and brought her to her feet. Everyone was watching, stunned and speechless. He led her to the middle of the room. Olive stumbled once, but he steadied her.

She tried to dance, but it was painful to watch. It was probably the first time in her life anyone had ever asked her to dance. She bounced around a lot, trying to imitate dancers she had

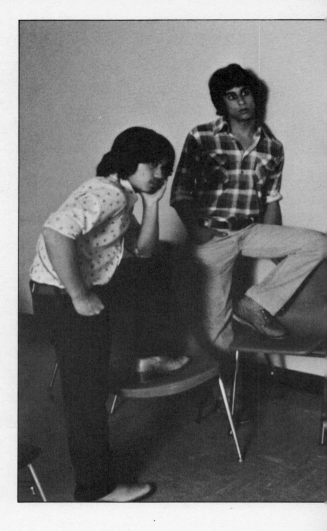

seen. Johnny didn't seem to notice. He acted like she was doing great.

Meanwhile, the guys in his group were watching all this with their mouths hanging open. They couldn't believe that Johnny was really dancing with Olive Tease. Before long, Hal Richmond decided that it was a joke. He figured that Johnny was having some fun, so he came onto the dance

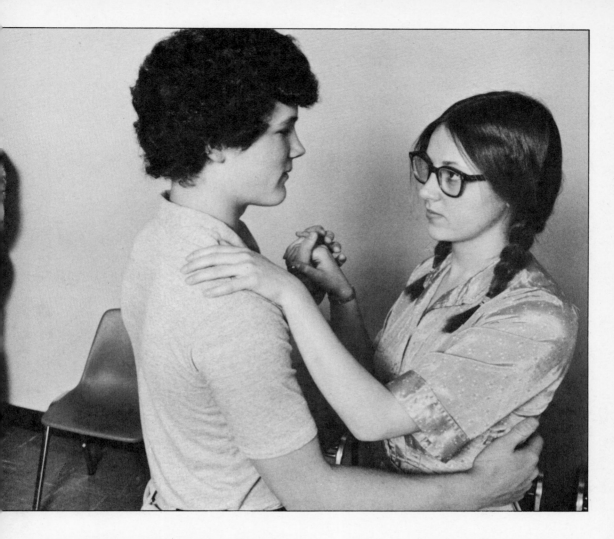

floor, grinning. He tapped Johnny on the shoulder to cut in.

Johnny stepped back, looking very surprised. Olive stopped dead in her tracks. She was frightened.

"My dance," Richmond said, giving Johnny a big wink.

Olive swallowed and tried to dance with Hal. Johnny walked off the floor and stood against the wall. He scowled as though wondering what was going on.

Mickey Catalano was next. He cut in on Richmond. "Come on, Hal," he said, "give a guy a break."

He didn't dance for more than a few seconds before another member of the group came over and tapped him on the shoulder. It was all very confusing to Olive, and there was a look of panic in her eyes.

The laughter started slowly — a snicker here and there as people realized what was going on. It was all a joke. The laughter spread.

Suddenly, Olive realized too. She stopped dancing and stood perfectly still in the middle of the floor. Just then, the needle squealed over the record, and the music broke off. Olive's eyes filled with tears. She turned around and looked hard at Johnny Miller.

"Why?" she said. Her voice was choked. "Why did you do this?"

Johnny looked stunned. He didn't know what to say.

"I never did anything to you," Olive went on. And then, with her eyes blazing, she shrieked, "I hate you!" She turned and ran out of the room.

You could "hear" the silence. Johnny stared at the floor. He couldn't believe what had happened. Ms. Mansfield broke the spell. "You're all wonderful," she said disgustedly. And she, too, slammed out of the room.

It was all over the school in a flash. Everybody was talking about the scene at the disco. I was in Mr. Johnson's fifth-period English class with Johnny, and he still looked bewildered.

Mr. Johnson was writing at his desk when there was a knock on the door. He opened the door, and Olive

was standing there. The room was silent. Every eye went to Johnny, then back to the door. We could only catch a few words of their hushed conversation: "Permission...talk to...highly irregular...the office said...." Mr. Johnson stepped back from the door to let Olive in.

No one moved a muscle. All eyes were fixed on Olive as she crossed in front of the class. Her sturdy shoes thumped on the wooden floor. We had no idea what she was going to do. But

it was obvious that she was heading for Johnny Miller.

She stopped in front of him. "I want to apologize," she said. "I know it wasn't your fault. You were just being kind. I was wrong to say I hated you. I'm sorry."

Johnny's mouth moved, but there was no sound. Olive had already turned and was heading for the door.

There was a single snicker, and then there was just silence.

She crossed back in front of the class. Her eyes glistened, but she held her head high. For a brief moment, she was absolutely beautiful. I never saw anything like it. She stopped at the door and thanked Mr. Johnson. He just nodded.

"Olive?" Johnny was on his feet. She paused with her hand on the door knob and looked back. "Thank you," he said.

There was a bare hint of a smile as Olive bowed her head. Then, she went out the door, closing it softly.

READING CHECK

WORD MEANING FROM CONTEXT

1. Johnny left his clique to dance with Olive. The word *clique* means ____.
   a. chair
   b. sound a clock makes
   c. close group of friends

2. When Johnny asked Olive to dance, all the other kids were stunned. The word *stunned* means ____.
   a. happy
   b. shocked
   c. mad

MAIN IDEA

3. Another title for this story could be ____.
   a. The Outsider
   b. Disco Dancing
   c. Joking Around

DETAILS

4. Give two reasons why Olive had no friends. _____

_____

_____

_____

_____

SEQUENCE

5. Olive got angry at Johnny after _____

_____.

FINDING PROOF

6. Olive had courage. Proof of this is _____

_____.

CAUSE AND EFFECT

7. Olive was upset when so many boys asked her to dance because

_____.

MAKING INFERENCES

8. Why did the kids think it was a joke when Johnny asked Olive to

dance? _____

9. How do you know that Johnny wasn't playing a joke on Olive?

_____

WHAT DO YOU THINK?

In what ways was Olive ''different'' from the other students? Why do you think Johnny asked her to dance? When Johnny saw what his friends were doing, should he have tried to stop them? Why did Olive feel she had to apologize to Johnny? What effect did her apology have on him? On the narrator? On the others?

CHARACTERIZATION

Do you think this story really happened? Do you think Olive and Johnny are real people? Probably not. But the author of the story wanted them to seem real. All authors try to make their characters "come alive."

To do this, authors have their characters think, talk, and act like real people. They have feelings — happiness, sadness, fear — just like we do. Authors even give their characters **motivations**, or reasons, for doing the things they do.

The problem is, authors don't always come right out and tell you what to think. Sometimes you have to read between the lines. You have to put things together and draw your own conclusions.

What made Olive tick? Follow the steps on the next few pages and see what you come up with. When you're done, you'll understand why she got so upset at the dance. And you'll know why she apologized to Johnny at the end.

Physical Appearance

1. What kind of clothes did Olive wear? _____

2. What kind of glasses did she wear? _____

3. How did she wear her hair? _____

What do you learn about Olive from her appearance? _____

_____

Personality Through Actions

1. Find two places in the story that show that Olive was a very shy

girl. _____

_____

2. The following sentences tell you something about Olive.
   "Olive stumbled once, but he steadied her."
   "It was probably the first time in her life that anyone had ever asked her to dance."

What do these statements tell you about her? _____

_____

3. What else do you learn about Olive from the following sentence?

"She bounced around a lot, trying to imitate dancers she had seen."

_____

_____

4. After many boys danced with her, Olive stopped. She turned to Johnny and said, ''Why did you do this? I never did anything to you...I hate you!'' This statement tells you something *new* about Olive. It's a side of her we hadn't seen before. What do her words tell you about her? Circle the letter of the best answer.

a. Olive is not afraid to say what she thinks.

b. Olive has a terrible temper.

c. She never liked Johnny because he was so popular.

5. At the end of the story, Olive apologizes to Johnny. This tells you even more about her. Why does she apologize? Circle the letter of the best answer.

a. She's afraid Johnny won't like her if she doesn't.

b. She's not too proud to admit she was wrong.

c. She wants the other kids to forgive her too.

Others' Views of Olive

The story is written from the point of view of a student. That means we see everything through the eyes of another student who was there. How others ''see'' Olive helps us to understand her better.

1. The narrator of the story said, ''If it weren't for Olive's goofy name, you'd never know she was alive.'' What does the narrator mean by this?

_____

_____

_____

_____

2. When the boys asked Olive to dance, the other kids began to laugh. This shows what they thought about Olive. Circle the letter of the best answer.

   a. They saw her as an object — not as a person with feelings.

   b. They didn't like the way she was dancing.

   c. They thought she was enjoying herself.

3. At the end, Olive apologized to Johnny. The narrator of the story said, "For a brief moment, she was absolutely beautiful." What did the narrator mean by this? Circle the letter of the best answer.

   a. Olive was dressed better than before.

   b. It really wasn't Olive who came into the room. It was a prettier girl.

   c. The narrator saw that she was a nice person on the inside. This seemed to change her appearance.

OK. You've just looked at Olive in many different ways. You've learned about her from her appearance, her actions, and her words. You've even seen her through the eyes of others.

Now it's your job to put all the pieces together. Write a brief paragraph. Tell what kind of person you think Olive was. Then, you'll be able to better understand why she did the things she did.

_____

_____

_____

_____

_____

PUNCTUATION

Tease, Olive was written in the teacher's roll book.
"Tease Olive" was written in the teacher's roll book.

The sentences above have the same words. But they have different meanings. One simply means that Olive's name was in the teacher's roll book. The other means that the teacher had made a note to play a joke on poor Olive. The difference is made by **punctuation**.

Below are pairs of questions and answers. The words in the questions are the same. But the meanings are different. Pay close attention to the way each question is punctuated. Then write the letter of the answer that matches each question. The first one is done for you.

__b__ 1. **Are you writing, Alice?**

__a__ 2. **Are you writing Alice?**

     a. No, I'll phone her instead.
     b. Yes, I'm writing my history report.

_____ 3. **Where is the book I lent you in the park?**

_____ 4. **Where is the book I lent you? in the park?**

     a. Yes, it is, but I'll go right back and find it.
     b. It's here on my desk.

_____ 5. **Is art the most important thing in your life?**

_____ 6. **Is Art the most important thing in your life?**

     a. Yes, I love him very much.
     b. Yes, I plan to be a painter when I get out of school.

_____ 7. **Would you like to see a man eating lion?**

_____ 8. **Would you like to see a man-eating lion?**

     a. Yes, if he cooked it himself.
     b. Yes, if it's in a cage.

_____ 9. **Where are you going with that honey?**

_____10. **Where are you going with that, honey?**

      a. I'm taking it back to the store.
      b. Wherever you want me to, sweetheart.

_____11. **Can Betty Lou and Tom ride in our car?**

_____12. **Can Betty, Lou, and Tom ride in our car?**

      a. Well, it will be pretty crowded with three more.
      b. Sure, she can sit on his lap.

_____13. **"Who likes fries?" asked Charles, covered with ketchup.**

_____14. **"Who likes fries," asked Charles, "covered with ketchup?"**

      a. I do, it's the only way I do like them.
      b. Here's a towel to wipe your face and hands.

_____15. **The teacher called the students names.**

_____16. **The teacher called the students' names.**
   a. He must have been pretty mad.
   b. He needed to take attendance.

_____17. **Are you sure Ann said our uncle is looking for a job?**

_____18. **"Are you sure Ann," said our uncle, "is looking for a job?"**

   a. Yes, he got tired of sleeping all day long.
   b. That's what she told me, Uncle Bill.

_____19. **What rat stole the winner's skates?**

_____20. **What rat stole the winners' skates?**

   a. Who knows? She says she left them right next to the
      garbage can.
   b. It had to be a big one to walk off with a dozen pairs.

MID-BOOK ACTIVITY

Select a character from one of the stories you've read in this book. Then pretend that he or she is being interviewed on a TV talk show. Answer each interview question *from the point of view of that character* — that is, as the character would have answered it.

Interview of: _____
(character's name)

Story title: _____

Interviewer: How do you feel about the way you are described or portrayed in the story?

Character: _____

_____

_____

Interviewer: What was your most difficult moment in the story?

Character: _____

_____

_____

Interviewer: What was going through your mind during this difficult time?

Character: _____

_____

Interviewer: How did you really feel about the other characters in the story?

Character: _____

_____

_____

Interviewer: Describe your strengths and weaknesses to the readers.

Character: _____

_____

_____

Interviewer: Would you like the readers to know other things about you that were not covered in the story? If so, describe these characteristics.

Character: _____

_____

_____

Interviewer: What are your feelings about the way your author ended the story?

Character: _____

_____

_____

VOCABULARY STUDY

beaten — struck; defeated
cemetery — a graveyard
century — a hundred years
chauffeur — a driver who works for someone else
committed — was done, did
failure — lack of success; a breakdown

foolishness — something silly
investigate — search; look into
mortician — one who takes charge of funerals and burying the dead; an undertaker
nervously — afraid or worried
portrait — a painting of a person
skidded — slid or slipped

Below are some sentences. Complete them by filling in the blanks with words from the list above. Then look at the letters in the squares. They will spell out **something a tired vampire might take**.

1. "I can't find any*body* in the funeral parlor!" said the

   absent-minded _ _ _ _ _ _ _ ☐ _ .

2. His poems were really bad. When he wrote a rhyme he

   ☐ _ _ _ _ _ _ _ _ a crime.

3. Like a _ □ _ _ _ _ _ _, I've been framed," said the criminal.

4. "Your □ _ _ _ _ _ _ _ _ _ _ pains me," said Aunt Abby when I put the tack in her chair.

5. Want to hear something deep and dark? There's been a power

□ _ _ _ _ _ _ in the cellar.

6. "If you □ _ _ _ _ _ _ _ _ _ _ my past, you'll find it was pretty hairy," said the skeleton of the gorilla.

7. "I'm all a flutter," said the ghost □ _ _ _ _ _ _ _ _.

8. "We just can't win, we always get □ _ _ _ _ _," said the egg.

9. "I've been around a lot in the last _ _ _ _ _ □ _," said the hundred-year-old fence.

10. "I've had a hard time in this _ □ _ _ _ _ _ _," said the gravestone.

11. "You'll drive me to the grave!" said the undertaker to his

_ _ □ _ _ _ _ _ _.

12. "Hair today, gone tomorrow," said the bald grave digger as his

wig _ □ _ _ _ _ _ off.

THE
DEAD PAST

A man visits a grave — and remembers. Sometimes, things that happened years ago can never be laid to rest.

THE DEAD PAST by Al Nussbaum

When he reached the grave, Felix Kurtz sat down on a nearby tombstone. He was tired. A new highway was going to cross the cemetery. The grave had to be moved, and Kurtz wanted to be there.

Fifty years had passed since the funeral. He hadn't visited the cemetery in all that time. But he had no trouble finding the old grave. Kurtz' life had been filled with success. It was easy to remember his only failure.

A truck turned into the cemetery. The truck was equipped for lifting heavy things. It bumped along the gravel road toward the old man.

Three workmen climbed down from the truck. One went to Kurtz. "Mr. Kurtz?" he said. "Which grave is it?"

Kurtz pointed to the grave.

The man bent over the tombstone. He ran his fingers over the dates. "After all this time, there isn't going to be much left," he said.

"Yes, there will," Kurtz said. "The coffin was cast iron. It took eight strong men to carry it...."

Emily Kurtz

Born
Oct 4, 1912
Died
Oct 3, 1929

As he waited, Kurtz remembered the day Myron Shay had come to Kurtzville. It was the time of the cave-in at the mine. Shay was an artist. His job was to make drawings for a newspaper in Washington, DC.

Kurtz didn't want anyone to investigate the conditions at the mine. So he hired Shay away from the newspaper. He paid him to paint a portrait of his sister Emily instead.

After some time, the newspaper lost interest in the Kurtz coal mine. And Kurtz had no reason to keep Shay around.

"I thought you were a trained artist," Kurtz said. Shay was standing in front of his desk. "I thought you said you had a lot of experience."

Shay shifted his weight from foot to foot. "Yes, sir. I work in clay, stone, oils...."

"Do you always spend over a month on one small job?" Kurtz cut in.

"Well, sir, I..."

"No matter, no matter," Kurtz said impatiently. "I want the painting completed by Friday of this week. I won't pay you for your services unless it is."

"Oh, I wouldn't think of charging you, sir," Shay said.

Kurtz frowned. "What do you mean?"

Shay moved his hands nervously.

"Your sister and I...Emily and I are in love. We wish to marry. I...I've come to ask for your blessing."

Kurtz stood and came around the desk. "*You* want to marry *my* sister?" he laughed.

"Yes, sir. I love her and —"

"Love her? Do you think you're the first man who's pretended to love my sister? Let me tell you that she is underage. And she has no funds of her own. So forget your foolishness!"

"Sir," Shay said. "I have no interest in money. I love your sister. She's a warm and sensitive human being."

"Enough!" Kurtz exploded. "I own this town and everything in it. I

suppose you think I'll offer you money to stay away from Emily. If you do, you are wrong.''

Kurtz grasped the artist's wrists in his hands. ''You have fifteen minutes. Pack your things and get out of town. If you do not leave, I'll have your fingers smashed. You'll never be able to hold a brush again.''

When Shay was gone, Kurtz motioned to a clerk. ''Telephone Miss Kurtz. Tell her to come down here right away,'' he said.

The man returned in a few minutes. ''She isn't at home, Mr. Kurtz. The maid said she went to sit for her portrait.''

Kurtz snatched his hat and ran out of the office. He stopped at the main gate and called for his car. Then he ordered two company policemen to come with him.

When they got to Shay's place, Shay and Emily were pulling away in an open car.

''Catch them! Cut them off!'' Kurtz shouted to his driver.

The driver pushed the accelerator to the floor. But the large sedan was unable to catch up to the smaller car. Kurtz pounded the dashboard with his fists. ''Stop them!'' he shouted.

All at once, gunshots rang out. Kurtz turned in amazement. One of

the policemen was leaning from the rear window with his weapon in his hand. Ahead of them, the small car slowed down and stopped.

Kurtz' car skidded to a stop behind it. All four men rushed forward. They found Myron Shay holding Emily in his arms. A red stain on her dress was growing larger.

Later, at the company hospital, Dr. Moreau questioned Kurtz. "How did it happen?"

"An accident..." Kurtz stammered. "Emily was running away with — that artist! One of my policemen thought that a crime had been committed."

"I suppose it was young Shay who was supposed to have the accident," the doctor hissed. "Like the other young men you had beaten when they showed an interest in your sister."

By now, the shock was wearing off. And Kurtz didn't like anyone talking back to him. "Look, you old pest, don't preach to me. You have two jobs here — taking care of the sick and burying the dead. Just see to your duties as doctor-mortician, that's all. Understand?"

"Yes, sir," the doctor said meekly. But his eyes narrowed in hatred.

Kurtz waved a finger under the doctor's nose. "What's my sister's condition?" he demanded. "How soon can she leave here?"

"The wound is not serious. But she has lost a lot of blood," Dr. Moreau said. "I wouldn't move her for at least a week. She must have complete rest. Then, if nothing goes wrong..."

Kurtz cut in. "Just see to it that nothing does," he snapped.

The following days were unhappy ones for Felix Kurtz. The news of Emily's accident had spread. Everywhere Kurtz went, he caught people sneering at him. They all knew that Kurtz had met with his first failure. They knew the artist had not been frightened away. Instead, he had practically moved into the hospital to be near Emily.

Then the unexpected happened. Ten days after the accident, Kurtz was called to the hospital. The doctor told him that Emily had died during the night. Kurtz raised the sheet and looked at the still form for a moment. Then he ordered Dr. Moreau to do what had to be done.

Myron Shay left town without going to the funeral. That proved that Kurtz had been right about him all along....

"Mr. Kurtz! Mr. Kurtz!" It was the chauffeur's voice. Kurtz opened his eyes as the chauffeur shook him. "They're ready to lift the coffin."

Kurtz joined the workmen at the open grave. Soon the old rusty coffin was being lifted into the open air.

Suddenly, the edge of the grave gave away under the truck's weight. The coffin swung away. It smashed into a headstone, and crashed to the ground.

The men on the truck stared open-mouthed at the coffin. Kurtz went to it and looked down. A two-foot section of the lid was broken. Kurtz looked inside to see the figure of a young woman. She was wearing the high-necked fashion of a half century before. One of her ears had been damaged by a piece of the lid. Kurtz touched it and his hands shook.

The ear was made of wax — like the rest of the dummy. It had been formed with loving care by the sensitive hands of an artist.

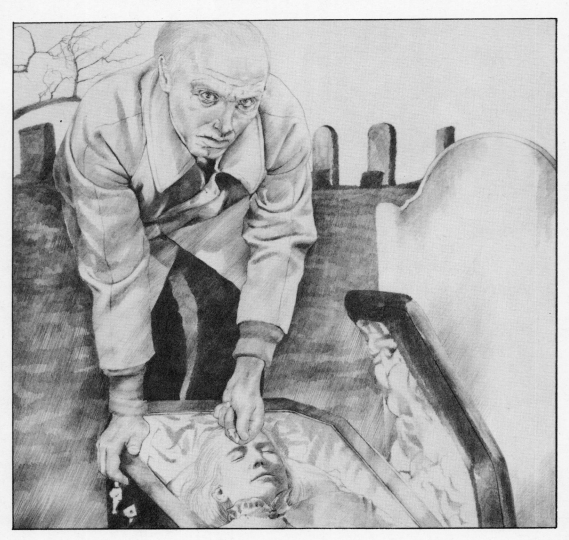

READING CHECK

WORD MEANING FROM CONTEXT

1. "The coffin was cast iron." In this story, the word *cast* means _____.
   a. given a part in a play
   b. thrown
   c. liquid poured into a mold and left to harden

2. The people in the town heard about the shooting. After that, they sneered at Kurtz. The word *sneered* means _____.
   a. looked with scorn and disapproval
   b. sneezed
   c. watched carefully

MAIN IDEA

3. The title of the story is "The Dead Past." Why is this an example of *irony*? (Remember: *irony* is the opposite of what you'd expect.)

_____

_____

DETAILS

4. Shay had first come to town to _____.

SEQUENCE

5. Shay left town after _____

_____

FINDING PROOF

6. Shay didn't turn up at the funeral. Kurtz *thought* this was proof

that _____ .

7. Dr. Moreau was on Emily's and Shay's side. Proof is that _____

_____ .

CAUSE AND EFFECT

8. Kurtz had Shay paint a portrait of Emily because _____

_____ .

MAKING INFERENCES

9. When the coffin broke and Kurtz saw that the ''body'' was made of
   wax, he probably wondered _____.
   a. ''Who did this?''
   b. ''Where have Emily and her husband been all these years?''
   c. ''Why did I get such a cheap coffin?''

WHAT DO YOU THINK?

What kind of person was Kurtz? Why didn't people like him? People in town said that Kurtz had failed only once. What did they mean? Why didn't Kurtz want his sister to marry Shay? What do you think Shay and Emily were doing when Kurtz chased after them? Why did Emily ''die'' after 10 days? Could she have ''died'' after two days? What part did Dr. Moreau play in Emily's and Shay's plan? Was he right to deceive Kurtz? What do you think went through Kurtz' mind when the coffin fell open? Do you think he'll try to find Shay and Emily now?

FLASHBACK

Did you notice? The story you just read wasn't written like most stories. The things that happened weren't told in the order that they really happened. The story, as you remember, begins in the present. It goes back 50 years. Then it come back to the present again. When writers do this, they are using **flashback**.

Flashback means exactly what it says it is. The writer *flashes* — goes quickly — to the past, or *back* in time. A writer may do this to help explain the action or feelings of a character. Without a *flashback* in this story, we would never understand the ending.

Below are statements about parts of the story. Number the parts in the order that they would have happened in life. Begin with the earliest event.

_____ The mine in Kurtzville caved in.

_____ Shay asked Emily to marry him.

_____ A highway was planned to be built across the cemetery.

_____ Emily was taken to the hospital.

_____ The coffin dropped from the truck and split open.

_____ Shay began to paint Emily's portrait.

_____ Kurtz was told that Emily died.

_____ Three men dug up Emily's coffin.

_____ A funeral was held for Emily.

Now go back and check the statements that are a part of the flashback.

Here is a mini-story. Read it carefully. Then number the statements that follow to show the order in which things happened in real life.

Sally's heart was pounding. What would her report card say? It made all the difference in the world to her.

Her last report card was still very clear in her mind. She would never forget the look on her father's face. His words still sent shivers down her back. "No more TV and no more phone calls at night," he said, "until these grades come up."

"Sally Bradley. Sally Bradley." Sally's teacher had been calling her name. She went up to the front of the room to get her report card. Her hands were shaking so much, she could hardly open it. Then she saw it! Written in big letters were one *A*, two *B*'s, and a *C*. "Congratulations, Sally," she said to herself. "You did it!"

_____ Sally's father is angry about her report card.

_____ She is nervous about getting her report card.

_____ Her report card tells her that she made good grades.

_____ Sally can't watch TV or talk on the phone.

Now, circle the statements that are part of a flashback. Why do you think the author used a flashback in this story? _____

_____

_____

_____

WHAT
DO
YOU KNOW?

What do ostriches do when they're scared? What happens when a bull sees red? Who was the Baby Ruth candy bar named after? If you think you know, you're in for some surprises.

VOCABULARY STUDY

actual — real, true
limits — boundaries; what you
  can't go beyond
misinformed — believing
  something that is wrong
popular — liked by many
recycled — used over again

sluggish — slow, dull; without
  much energy
victim — person something bad
  happens to
wilderness — wild place where
  no one lives

Words that mean the opposite of other words are called **antonyms**. Sometimes you can create an antonym by adding a prefix, like *un-* or *dis-* or *mis-*. Sometimes you need a whole other word.

The sentences below don't make sense. But, by changing one word, you can make them clear. Replace each underlined word with its antonym from the list above.

1. Do you think a bicycle made of new materials will go just as fast as

   one made of <u>new</u> materials? _____

2. They call me Tommy, but my <u>false</u> name is Thomas.

   _____

3. Carol can have seven dates a week, if she wants them. She is the

   most <u>disliked</u> girl in school. _____

4. George is <u>right</u> when he says that goats can fly.

   _____

5. The police comforted the <u>criminal</u> after the crime.

   _____

6. Ellen loves to wander through the <u>city</u>, where the trees are tall and green, and you never hear a human voice. _____

7. You just can't make my brother wake up in the morning. He's <u>lively</u> until almost noon. _____

8. It's against the law to keep elephants as pets within the <u>freedom</u> of the city. _____

WHAT DO YOU KNOW?

Do you know which of these statements are true?

- *Thomas Edison invented the first light bulb.*
- *India ink comes from India.*
- *Ostriches stick their heads in the sand to hide from danger.*
- *Rapidly boiling water is a lot hotter than slowly boiling water.*

If you said they are *all* true, most people would agree with you. But you would still be wrong, according to *The Dictionary of Misinformation*, by Thomas Burnam.

Professor Burnam says that a lot of us are misinformed about these and many other popular beliefs. He says that a lot of "facts" have been passed down incorrectly for years. So he wrote a book to set the facts straight. He also explains how a lot of the wrong ideas got started in the first place.

The book is called a "dictionary" because the subjects it covers are listed in alphabetical order — like the words in a dictionary. But this book is a lot more fun to read. It is made up of 764 very short articles about things everybody knows — but incorrectly.

Here are some examples from the book. Some of them may surprise you.

- **Bulls** charge when they see red. Wrong, says Professor Burnam. The color is *not* what makes the bull charge. Scientific studies have shown that bulls can't tell one color from another.

- **The light bulb** was invented by Thomas A. Edison. Not really. Others had been working on light bulbs for years. A French scientist Jean Foucault made an arc light in 1844, three years before Edison was born. An Englishman Sir Joseph Swan turned on his lamp in 1860. Edison's light bulb wasn't "invented" until 1879.

- **Moss** grows on the north side of trees. True, it often does. But this won't help you tell direction if you get lost. Why not? Because in most places moss grows on the north, south, east, and west sides of trees.

- **India ink** comes from China. It always has. So it really should be called "China ink." It is called that in France.

- **Wolves** are dangerous. They often form large packs to kill and eat people lost in the wilderness. Actually, there is not a single proven case of wolves attacking a human in North America. And wolves almost never get together in large groups — to eat people or anything else.

- **Ostriches** do *not* stick their heads in the sand, for any reason. The other idea has been around for thousands of years — even though scientists have always said it isn't true.

- **Frankenstein** is *not* the name of a monster. That is the name of the man who created the monster in a book written by Mary Shelley in 1818.

- **Catgut** is made from the insides of sheep — *not* cats.

- **Water** boils at 212°F. Rapidly boiling water is *no* hotter than slowly boiling water.

- **Babe Ruth**, the famous baseball player, did *not* have a candy bar named after him. The Baby Ruth candy bar is named after a baby whose name was Ruth.

• **Chop suey** was *not* invented in China. It was first served in a California mining camp. A Chinese cook threw together some leftovers. He called it, *tsa sui*, which is a Chinese phrase meaning *a mixture of things*. The miners thought he was saying *chop suey*.

• **Goats** will eat anything, including tin cans. That's what most people think. But according to the author, even goats refuse to eat some things. They will nibble on almost anything, but they will not eat tin cans.

• **Camels** store water in their humps. Actually, the humps are fat, which is stored-up energy, just like fat is in humans. Camels do not "store" water anywhere. They can go without water for a long time because they sweat very little and their bodies keep recycling the water already in their systems.

• **Double-jointed** people can do tricks. No one is truly double-jointed. Some people can do "impossible" tricks with their arms and legs. That's because their ligaments are looser than those of other persons. Ligaments are muscle tissue that connect bones and hold body organs in place.

• **Lightning** never strikes twice in the same place. In fact, it often strikes the same place over and over again. Why? Because lightning is electricity, which "looks" for a good conductor to "run through." Air is a poor conductor. Trees, flagpoles, tall metal buildings, and people are better conductors. So lightning jumps out of the air and into whatever conductor is handy. If something was a good conductor once, it will be again, and again, and again. So look out!

• **The telephone** was *not* invented by Alexander Graham Bell. A German scientist named Phillip Reis invented a telephone 15 years before Bell put together his. Many other scientists also claim credit for inventing the phone. It took Bell several years in court to get an American patent on his "invention." Bell's phone worked better than the others — but it was not the first.

• **Bears** hibernate. Bears are *not* true hibernators. Bears do become sluggish and sleep in cold weather, but they do not hibernate. When an animal hibernates, its temperature, heart rate, and breathing rate drop to very low levels. Such low levels have not been recorded in bears.

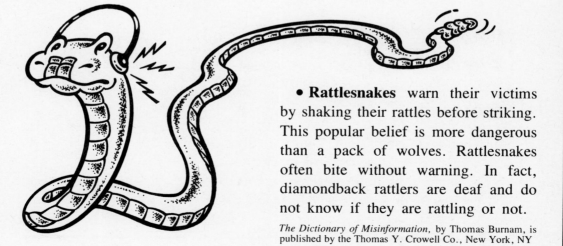

• **Rattlesnakes** warn their victims by shaking their rattles before striking. This popular belief is more dangerous than a pack of wolves. Rattlesnakes often bite without warning. In fact, diamondback rattlers are deaf and do not know if they are rattling or not.

The Dictionary of Misinformation, by Thomas Burnam, is published by the Thomas Y. Crowell Co., New York, NY

READING CHECK

WORD MEANING FROM CONTEXT

1. As used here, the word *article* means _____.
   a. something for sale
   b. a part of speech
   c. something written about a special subject

2. Bell got an American patent on his invention. The word *patent* means _____.
   a. a kind of soft leather
   b. an inventor's sole right to make, use, or sell his invention
   c. award

MAIN IDEA

3. *The Dictionary of Misinformation* is _____.
   a. a joke book
   b. a book of facts about women
   c. a book that lists and corrects wrong ideas people have had

DETAILS

4. The Baby Ruth candy bar is named after _____.

SEQUENCE

5. Thomas Edison's light bulb was invented _____.
   a. before Sir Joseph Swan's lamp
   b. at the time he discovered lightning
   c. after both Swan's and Foucault's lights

CAUSE AND EFFECT

6. India ink should be called China ink because _____

_____ .

7. Thomas Burnam's book is called a dictionary because _____

_____ .

FINDING PROOF

8. Wolves are not dangerous to human beings. Proof of this is

_____ .

MAKING INFERENCES

9. Scientists say that bulls are color-blind. Yet bull-fighters wave red-lined capes at them because _____.
   a. the red lining keeps the fighter warm
   b. the bull charges because the cape is in motion — and red looks good to the audience
   c. only red cloth is sold in countries which allow bull-fighting

WHAT DO YOU THINK?

Before you read the article, did you believe any of the things it says are not true? Can you think of other things people believe that you know are wrong? What are they? How do you think stories like these get started?

LOOK IT UP!

When you want information about a certain subject, you might go to a library. In the card catalog, in alphabetical order, are the titles of books on many subjects. How can you decide *which* book to take out? Which one will tell you exactly what you want to know?

Try your hand at these make-believe examples. Read about each person's topic. Then help the person evaluate the books he or she finds. To answer the questions, use only the letter of each book.

1. **Alice loves old movies. She wants to know all about the life of Hette Shearer, a famous star of the 1930's and 1940's. She looks under SHEARER, Hette, and finds:**

   a. *My Life in the Movies: An Autobiography*, by Hette Shearer.
   b. *Misery with Mother, the Great Shearer*, by Bonna Shearer Maller.
   c. *Hette Shearer: The Star I Loved*, by Peverell Pym, cameraman, HRS Studios.
   d. *The Science of Stardom: What Made Hette Shearer a Star?* by Willard Stodgely, Ph.D., Professor of Psychology, Brainyard University.

Which of these books would be likely to give the most flattering picture of Hette? _____

Which would give the least flattering picture? _____

Which might best explain her life? _____

Which is most accurate? _____

2. **Geroop lives on Mars in the year 4325 A.D. He found some old Earth rock records in a museum. Now he is crazy to know all about rock music. Under EARTH: ANCIENT MUSIC, in the Mars National Library, he finds tapes of old Earth books and magazines. But he can use them only for an hour. This is what he finds:**

a. Back issues of *Rock 'n Roll Magazine*, 1960–1979.
b. *The Rolling Stones: A Loving Tribute*, by Tim Outamynd.
c. *The Beatles: Voices of a Troubled Time*, by Professor Sylvia Scoller, Nuckle University.
d. Back issues of *The New York Times Music Section*, 1960–1979.

Which will tell Geroop how people who loved rock felt about it? ____

Which will tell him how rock music fit into its time? ____

Which will help him understand rock groups best? ____

3. **Tom has a new kitten. He wants to know how to take care of it and what to expect as it grows. Under CATS he finds:**

   a. *Cats I Have Known and Laughed At*, by Felina Farr of Pets, Inc.
   b. *How To Raise a Healthy Cat*, by Vicki Vett, Doctor of Veterinary Science.
   c. *What Sign Was Your Cat Born Under?* by Trolla Aster.
   d. *The Cat in History*, by Sherman Firman.

Which book would tell Tom what he wants to know? _____

Which book would tell him the most about cats in general? _____

Which book might be the funniest? _____

4. **Kim is interested in World War I — its causes, battles, and place in history. Under WORLD WAR I she finds:**

   a. *History of World War I*, by Lew Kendle, Professor of History, U.S. Military Academy. Copyright 1923.
   b. *Grandfather's War*, by Angela Brock, Professor of History, Princard University, granddaughter of the Chief of Staff of American forces during World War I. Copyright 1979.
   c. *Here in the Trenches*, by Sgt. H.G. Riggs. Copyright 1917.
   d. *Our Side Was Right!*, by Franz Kopplheim, former colonel in the German Army. Copyright 1919.

Which book is likely to give the most complete picture of the war in history? _____

Which book is most likely to give an American general's view as well as a long look at history? _____

Which book will tell how America's enemies felt? _____

Which book will give the most personal, first-hand view? _____

IT'S NOT EASY TO TEACH ETHICS

Teachers encourage students to use what they learn in their own lives. But who would expect the lunchroom to be a setting for a history lesson?

VOCABULARY STUDY

clutch   ethics   medal   politician   yelped

confess   furious   muscle   screecher   y'know

disgusting   guidance   okay   tightened

The sentences below all have to do with food or eating. Complete them with words from the list above. When you are done, the words in the squares will answer this question:

What did the egg say to the egg beater?

1. Juan ☐ _ _ _ _ _ when his foot touched the raw egg in his shoe.

2. The _ ☐ _ _ _ _ _ _ _ _ made a campaign speech at the dinner.

3. It's _ _ _ _ ☐ _ _ _ _ _ to watch someone put ketchup on apple pie.

4. I won a gold ☐ _ _ _ _ in the cooking contest.

5. I need some _ _ _ _ ☐ _ _ _ in planning tomorrow's menu.

6. It's _ ☐ _ _ with me if you cook fish for dinner.

7. My kid brother is a real _ _ _ ☐ _ _ _ _ _ if you take away his candy.

8. Eating spinach is supposed to build strong ☐ _ _ _ _ _s.

9. I _ _ _ _ ☐ _ _ that I ate the cookies you were saving for later.

10. If you have any _ ☐ _ _ _ _, you won't steal the peaches from that tree.

11. "You can't have it!" I cried and _ _ _ ☐ _ _ _ _ _ my hold on the apple.

12. If you don't try my oyster stew, I'll be _ _ _ ☐ _ _ _.

13. Let the others have some pretzels. Don't ☐ _ _ _ _ _ the bowl to you.

14. _'☐ _ _ _, you're as sweet as sugar.

IT'S NOT EASY TO TEACH ETHICS

by Stuart James

It's crazy how things get out of hand. I mean, you start off with a simple little thing. Then, all of a sudden, there's all sorts of heavy stuff coming down. Mr. DiMoyne had nothing to do with it, but I think he got the worst of it.

We were in the lunchroom and Bernie Sachs started playing "disgusting." This is a game where you have to think of the most disgusting thing you can imagine for dessert. No dirty stuff or four-letter words are allowed. I could tell you some of the winners, but they might just gross you out.

It is not my favorite game. But I have to admit that Bernie Sachs is the All-Time Gold Medal Champion of "disgusting." And when Agnes Varda is there, it *is* kind of funny. Agnes is a screecher.

"Liver-flavored ice cream," Bernie said, "topped with crushed blood-shot eyeballs and...."

Agnes screeched. She covered her ears and bounced up and down in her chair. She loved it.

Bernie was just warming up. A few other people had a try, then the World's Champion topped his all-time low, if you know what I mean.

Agnes was raising her hamburger

when she screamed. The hamburger flew out of her hand and landed on the front of Jill Barnoff's white jacket. There was a great splash of ketchup. Jill yelped. She jumped out of her chair, throwing a cup of cola into the air. Harvey Manners leaped out of the way and crashed into a kid passing the table with a loaded tray. The contents were dumped on the next table.

The scene was incredible. There were people leaping everywhere and screaming. Margo Cirrillo got a bowl of chicken soup right over her head. She sat there, howling, her eyes shut and her head covered with noodles.

I never saw so much food flying through the air — ketchup, hamburgers, french fries, cola, milk. Even a table was overturned. And it all happened in less than a minute. A whole corner of the lunchroom was a mess.

Poor Mr. DiMoyne had guard duty. He came running. The newspaper he had been reading was clutched in his hand. He stopped at the edge of the mess. "What happened?"

Agnes was completely rattled. "He said..." And she shouted out the name of Bernie's new World Champion dessert. A lot of people said, "Eccchhh!" Mr. DiMoyne made a face.

"Who said that?" Mr. DiMoyne asked.

"He did."

The chair next to me was empty. The Gold Medalist had left. Split. Gone. Mr. DiMoyne was looking at me.

"Who said it, Bonnie?"

"It wasn't me!" I shouted.

It always happens. At a really serious time like that I see something funny. I looked up and there was Margo still covered with noodles. I laughed.

"What's funny? Mr. DiMoyne demanded.

"Nothing," I said, but I couldn't stop laughing.

"Why are you laughing?"

"I'm not." What I really meant was that I didn't *want* to be laughing. The way things were going, I didn't

think anything was funny. Mr. Di-Moyne was furious and getting madder by the second.

"What?" he asked.

"I mean yes. No. I mean no."

I was getting completely rattled. "I mean *I* didn't say it." I looked hard at my shoes and tightened all the muscles in my face. The laughing turned into a kind of horrible smile.

I had to admire the way Mr. Di-Moyne was managing to control himself. He swung back to Agnes and pointed at me. "Was it Bonnie?"

Poor Agnes. She realized that she had already said too much. She didn't want to get anybody into trouble. "No," she said.

"Who, then?"

"I don't know," Agnes said.

This brought Mr. DiMoyne back to me. "You know..." I began. "I..." This was a tough one. I wasn't going to lie to Mr. DiMoyne. I have him for history and he's my favorite teacher. I mean, he really believes all the stuff he teaches. If a politician gets caught stealing, for example, it ruins his whole day. I admire him. On the other hand, I wasn't going to mention Bernie Sach's name.

"Who was it?" Mr. DiMoyne repeated.

"I..." I hated to go on. I knew he was going to have a fit. "I can't say."

What a look he gave me! "Let's go," he said. He motioned his head toward the door. I got up from my chair and followed.

We went down the hall. Mr. Di-Moyne stayed about three paces ahead of me. I followed him into the Guidance Center. He then nodded for me to take a seat.

There is a row of small cubicles where you sit to wait for a guidance counselor. You can't see or talk to the person in the next cubicle. The kids call it Death Row. I sat down. Mr. DiMoyne went to the desk and spoke to Mrs. Barnard who gave me her "what-have-you-done-now" look. She pointed to one of the conference room doors.

Mr. DiMoyne gave me the head motion again, and I got up. He held the door for me to enter, then closed it after us.

"Sit," he ordered. I took a chair at the end of the conference table. He paced a few seconds. Then he said, "You are going to tell me who said that."

"Mr. DiMoyne, I can't."

He went to the other end of the table and wrapped his hands around the back of a chair. "I'm surprised that you are involved in this. I always thought better of you." He went on like that for a while, making me feel like a rat. "...a terrible thing to say."

"Mr. DiMoyne," I said. "I don't think it was really all that bad."

I got that look again. "At lunch?" he said.

"Well...I guess it's not the greatest thing I ever heard, but kids don't really mind."

"*Who* said it?" he asked again.

For a minute there, I thought he was going to be reasonable. I was wrong. "Mr. DiMoyne," I said, "I just can't tell you."

He stood there, leaning on a chair. His jaw worked back and forth. Finally he said, "You're asking to be expelled."

Oh, boy. I could just hear my parents. They would shout for 10 minutes before I even got a word in. I looked down at my hands. The only sound was Mr. DiMoyne's breathing.

"You don't think there is anything wrong with what was said?" he asked.

"I really don't, Mr. DiMoyne."

"Then why won't you say who said it?" His mouth was beginning to look a little white around the edges.

"First, I'll have to ask him if it's okay," I explained.

"Why?" he exploded.

"Ethics, Mr. DiMoyne, ethics!"

It was a cheap shot. I knew it when I said it.

Mr. DiMoyne looked as though I had just stabbed him. It was so unfair. For the past week, his class had been discussing ethics. You couldn't budge him on the subject of ethics. I could hear him saying: "Ethics are the principles that people live by. They are the values that govern individual and group conduct."

He relaxed his grip on the chair and

stood up. He took a deep breath. It was a lousy thing for me to do. Here he was, talking about democracy and world affairs. I was talking about ketchup and hamburgers. It's really a dirty trick to expect a teacher to be a saint.

"Hey, Mr. DiMoyne, I'm sorry." I stood up. "I'll take all the blame."

He just turned and went to the door and opened it. I followed him.

"Mr. DiMoyne, I'll confess. Go ahead. Expel me. I did it."

He didn't even bother to turn around. He walked past Death Row, out the door, and down the hall. His shoulders were a little slumped.

"Hey, Mr. DiMoyne," I said mostly to myself. "I'm sorry. I take it all back." But he didn't even hear me.

It was really heavy. Y'know, I'll bet it's not easy to teach ethics.

READING CHECK

WORD MEANING FROM CONTEXT

1. In this story, the word *ethics* means _____.
   a. doing what you believe is right
   b. a book by a famous writer
   c. a special high school course

2. In this story, the word *gross* means _____.
   a. big
   b. disgusting
   c. twelve dozen

MAIN IDEA

3. This story is about someone who _____

   _____.

DETAILS

4. It was fun to have Agnes present when Bernie played his game because she was _____.

SEQUENCE

5. Mr. DiMoyne talked about ethics in class _____.
   a. before the game in the lunchroom
   b. after the game in the lunchroom
   c. while the students were at lunch

FINDING PROOF

6. Bernie Sachs was afraid of getting in trouble. Proof is that he

_____.

CAUSE AND EFFECT

7. What happened as a result of Bernie's game? _____

_____

MAKING INFERENCES

8. Why did Mr. DiMoyne decide not to punish Bonnie? _____

_____

WHAT DO YOU THINK?

Do you think the name of the "new dessert" was bad enough to get someone in trouble? Or was it just fun? If the kids didn't mind it, should Mr. DiMoyne have cared? Why did things get "out of hand" in the lunchroom? Why do you think Mr. DiMoyne was mad?

If you were in Bonnie's place, would you have told on Bernie? Was saving Bernie worth getting expelled from school? Was it an unfair choice to make? Was the narrator right for not getting Bernie in trouble? Was she taking her history lesson one step too far? What did she mean when she said, "Mr. DiMoyne had nothing to do with it, but I think he got the worst of it"?

CONTEXT CLUES

When you read, you may come across words you do not know. If there's a dictionary handy, there's no problem. But what if there's no dictionary at hand? Many times it's possible to guess what a word means just from the way it's used in a sentence.

For example:

"There is a row of small *cubicles* where you sit to wait for a guidance counselor."

You read this sentence in "It's Not Easy to Teach Ethics." You might not know the word *cubicle*. But take a guess. Look at the meanings below. Choose the one that best defines *cubicle*.

      a. a unit of measurement
      b. part of a fingernail
      c. a small, enclosed area

If you chose *c*, you're right. From the clues in the sentence, you could say that a *cubicle* is a small enclosed area.

The words in the sentences that follow are probably unfamiliar words. But you can guess or infer their meanings. Read each sentence. Then write what you think each boldface word means.

1. Ed claims he saw a UFO, but I think it's **dubious**. He hasn't always told the truth before. _____

2. May and Lew are always fighting, but I think it's her fault. She's the **pugnacious** one. _____

3. I didn't want to argue, so I just made an **innocuous** remark when the subject came up. _____

4. I'd like to take that job, but the **remuneration** is so small I couldn't live on it. _____

5. Ellen would like to do as well in her new job as her **predecessor** in it did. _____

6. "You shall not stop me," cried the villain, "I will not be **thwarted** in my plans!" _____

7. Aunt Maggie said Claude was **impertinent** when he told her she was silly. _____

8. If you are **prudent**, you'll put away some of that money for a rainy day. _____

9. Our lawyer is rather **sagacious** when it comes to tax problems.

   _____

10. I'm feeling so **indolent** today that I don't think I can get up and play tennis. _____

11. Before I sign up for that course, I have to read the **prospectus** to see if it will interest me. _____

12. I can understand their **anguish** when they learned their child had been hurt. _____

13. Sam is always bored with things. But his sister has a very **inquisitive** nature. _____

14. The professor likes to **peruse** old books by candlelight.

   _____

15. Rosa is **adept** at wood-carving. The animals she carves look real.

    _____

16. If you're hungry, go to the Blotto Restaurant. They serve the most **copious** portions of food in town. _____

17. Let go of my skates — I won't **relinquish** them!

    _____

18. No matter how angry and upset Cheryl gets, she has a quiet, calm **demeanor**. _____

19. Karl loves all kinds of people. He's the most **gregarious** person I know. _____

20. Not a blade of grass grows in the desert because it is so **arid**.

_____

21. Joyce lives a **vagrant** life, wandering from Europe to Asia to Africa and back. _____

22. The best candidate lost the election because some lying person told **mendacious** stories about him. _____

You may not know the 16 boldface words in the two letters below. But don't worry. Following the letters is a list of meanings. From reading the letters, see if you can match the words with their definitions. Write the number of the right meaning above each boldface word. The first one is done for you.

Dear Mr. I.M. Knott:

I need to know what the stars say about my life. So I looked through the yellow pages of the telephone **directory**. I wanted to find an **astrologer** who could help me **interpret** my **horoscope**.

I found your name under HORO, so I am writing this **missive** to ask for **succor**. I need help because I am **bewildered**. Here's why:

I was born on August 2, so you are **cognizant** of the fact that I am a Leo. But I am **desperately** in love with a Pisces, born on March 16. I know that these two signs are supposed to be **incompatible**. But is it at all **conceivable** that we might find **connubial** happiness? Any **illumination** you shed on this subject would be accepted with deep **gratitude**.

> Thank you,
> Sandy Starstruck

Dear S. Starstruck:

Sorry, but you've got the wrong guy. If you ever need your watch fixed, I'll **accommodate** you. I'm a **horologist**.

> Starry-eyed,
> I.M. Knott

Definitions:

1. letter
2. mixed up
3. possible
4. chart of person's birth signs
5. thanks
6. do what is asked
7. light
8. person who studies the stars
9. madly
10. help
11. explain meaning of
12. book telling where to find things
13. aware of
14. having to do with marriage
15. one who makes, repairs, or sells clocks and watches
16. don't get along

VOCABULARY STUDY

ancient	customs	Martians	planet	switched
continue	harmful	ordinary	situation	system
creature	knowledge	physical	superior	

A letter from outer space is making the rounds in your school. Fill in the spaces with words from the list above to see what the letter says. The letters in the squares will tell who received the letter.

Life on Mars is never _ _ _ ☐ _ _ _ _. We

_ _ _ ☐ _ _ _ _ are ☐ _ _ _ _ _ _ _

beings. We are proud of our _ _ ☐ _ _ _ _ _ beauty

and our wonderful _ _ _ _ ☐ _ _ and traditions. We

_ _ _ _ _ _ ☐ _ to grow wiser all the time. But we never

forget what was handed down from _ _ _ _ _ _ ☐ times.

No ☐ _ _ _ _ _ _ or cruel _ _ _ ☐ _ _ _ _

lives on our lovely _ _ _ _ _ ☐. We all get along, and

our ☐ _ _ _ _ _ of government is ideal. We have great

_ _ _ ☐ _ _ _ _ _ on every subject. It's as if all the

lights of the universe had been _ _ _ _ _ ☐ _ _ on

to make our _ _ _ _ _ _ _ ☐ _ the best in all history.

THE EYES
HAVE IT

All the Council members were from the same planet — all except one. But which one? Joseph Heidel figured a way to find out. Then he set his plan into action....

THE EYES HAVE IT by James McKimmey

Joseph Heidel looked slowly around the dinner table at the five Council members. He hid his sharp look behind a screen of smoke from his cigar. He was the President of the Superior Council. It was the most important post on the occupied planet of Mars. Heidel had held the position for six years.

His fingers tapped the table. One. Two. Three. Four. Five. Five top people, each chosen and screened on Earth to take charge of the government of Mars.

Heidel's eyes flicked from one to another. Which one? Who was the imposter? Which one was not from Earth? Which one was the Martian?

Sara Sadler's dry voice cut through the silence. "This is not just an ordinary meeting, then, Mr. President?"

Heidel stared into Sadler's eyes. "No, Sara, it isn't. This is a very special meeting. This is where we take the clothes off the sheep and find the wolf."

Heidel watched the five faces. Sadler, Meehan, Locke, Forbes, Clark. One of them. Which?

"I don't understand you," said Harry Locke.

"No, of course not," Heidel said. "I'll explain." It was the kind of situation he handled best—full of excite-

ment and suspense.

"Here it is," he said. "We have an imposter among us—a spy." He waited, letting his words sink in. Then he leaned back in his chair. "Tonight," he said, "I am going to expose this imposter—right here, at this table."

He searched the faces for a telltale movement, a flash in an eye. But there was none.

"One of us, you say," Bob Clarke said.

"That's right, Bob," said Heidel.

"Quite a situation," said Joan Forbes with a faint smile.

Bob Clarke cleared his throat. "May I ask, sir, how this was discovered? And why you are sure the spy is a member of the Superior Council?"

"Of course," Heidel said. "There's no need to go into the troubles we've been having. You all know about that. How these troubles started is the important thing. Remember the business about the social workers?"

"They were going to change the family patterns and school system of the whole planet for us," John Meehan said.

"Right," Heidel said. "But then sixty-seven social workers were killed."

"I remember the Martian note of apology," said Joan Forbes. "*We have raised and taught our children in*

our own way for 200,000 years. We prefer to continue, thank you. They had their nerve, didn't they?"

"That's not important," Heidel said. "The point is that no one knew that those sixty-seven men and women were social workers when they went into the Martian settlements. No one, that is, except myself and you five people. They were killed before they had spoken a word to a single Martian."

Heidel looked around the table. "There is no use going into the other incidents," he said. "You remember them all."

Then he pounded his fist on the table. "Each of our efforts to give these people something good from Earth was cut off at the source. And *we* are the source. Only a leak in the Superior Council could have caused it. One of us here is responsible, and I am going to find out who."

The five people waited.

"Kessit!" Heidel called.

A gray-haired butler in a black coat came in.

"We'll have our coffee now," Heidel said. The man nodded, and a few minutes later brought in coffee in china cups.

Heidel smiled as he stirred his coffee. He lifted the cup, took a sip, and smacked his lips. "Ah, excellent," he said. "A fresh blend from Earth."

The others lifted their cups and drank.

Suddenly, Heidel had a pistol in his hand. "Now I'll tell you my plan," he said. "As you know, Dr. Kingly, the head of our research laboratory, died a few days ago. But before he died, he made a discovery. The discovery answered a question that has puzzled Earth people ever since we became rulers of Mars. Is there really any difference between an Earth person and a Martian? There never seemed to be any physical difference. But Dr. Kingly proved that there is."

The five people drank their coffee silently.

"Dr. Kingly was...examining the body of a dead Martian," Heidel went on.

"You mean an autopsy?" Forbes asked, shocked. "That's against the ancient Martian Law."

Heidel shrugged. "Every law is broken from time to time," he told her. "Anyway, Dr. Kingly had discovered a solution that gave him more time to work on a body. He injected it into the bloodstream —"

"The bloodstream!" said Forbes.

"Yes," said Heidel. "It had to be done before the Martian was dead."

"That means that Kingly murdered the Martian so he could work on him," Forbes said.

Heidel's fingers closed around the handle of the pistol. "Hush up,

Joan," he scolded. "Let me continue."

Heidel cleared his throat, then went on. "Dr. Kingly had injected the solution and left the Martian on the table in the lab. He came back at night. It was dark. But before he switched on the lights, he saw a glow. The eyes of the dead Martian were glowing in the dark like a pair of hot coals."

"Weird," said Sadler.

"Dr. Kingly," said Heidel, "had

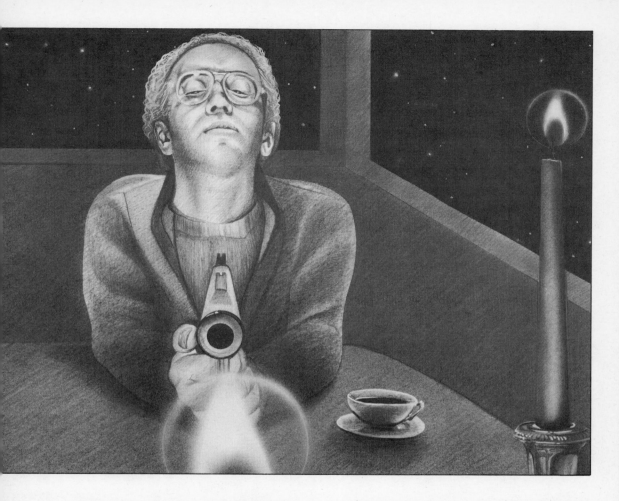

discovered that there *is* a difference between an Earth person and a Martian. It is in the eyes. When the solution is injected into an Earth person, nothing happens. But in a Martian, it causes the eyes to light up. Kingly went on testing, and found that Martians can see in the dark. They've kept us from finding it out all these years. Their eyes are different from ours.''

Heidel lifted the pistol. ''I have won prizes for my marksmanship,'' he said proudly. ''Now, I am going to shoot out the four candles on this table. When the candles are out, we will have darkness. And then we will find our Martian rat. Because, you see, I have added Dr. Kingly's solution to our coffee. No taste. No harmful effects—except to one person in this room.''

Heidel aimed his pistol at the first candle. ''I have five bullets in this gun,'' he said. ''Four for the candles.

And one for the creature whose eyes light up when the last candle goes out.''

A shot rang out.

''One,'' said Heidel. He stopped to let the suspense build. ''You know, I wonder how the guilty one of you pulled it off. You were all so carefully screened on Earth...''

''Sir, I don't really think it would have been too hard,'' Joan Forbes said, after a moment. ''Suppose the Martians kidnapped someone going back to Earth. They could have then put one of their own on the rocket in that person's place. Some Martians are pretty clever, you know. Earth people have taught them a lot. Suppose they studied and learned the customs of Earth. Suppose they found ways to change some records and some pictures. It's a long way from here to dear old Earth. Communication isn't too good. It might not have been so difficult.''

''Hmm,'' said Heidel. He raised the pistol again. Another shot echoed in the room. ''Two,'' he said. ''What you say may make sense, Forbes. But it doesn't say why. We tried to give

these Martians everything—our culture, our knowledge, our beliefs. Why would they turn it all down?"

"Maybe they just don't like our TV shows," Sadler said dryly.

Heidel's mouth twisted. He fired the third and fourth shots quickly, one after the other. The room shook with the sound. Then there was total darkness. And silence—except for the gasp that escaped Heidel's lips.

"Well," said Joan Forbes finally. "There it is. Quite a surprise, isn't it?"

Heidel clung to the pistol, feeling his hands grow clammy. He looked around the table. What he saw were *five* pairs of glowing eyes.

"Yes, all of us," said Meehan.

"I still have one bullet left," Heidel said in a shaky voice. He squinted into the darkness.

"It won't do you much good," Forbes said. "We have you covered. And remember, we can see *you* perfectly, as if it were broad daylight."

Heidel jumped as a hand brushed his shoulder. "Care for more coffee, sir?" asked the butler. "I, too, can see in the dark."

READING CHECK

WORD MEANING FROM CONTEXT

1. Mars was an occupied planet. The word *occupied* means _____.
   a. busy
   b. taken over by the enemy
   c. lived in

2. The Council members had been "screened" on Earth. This means _____.
   a. they were protected from evil forces
   b. they had been motion picture stars
   c. they had passed a series of tests and examinations

3. An *imposter* is someone who _____.
   a. tries to deceive others
   b. tries to help others
   c. wants to entertain others

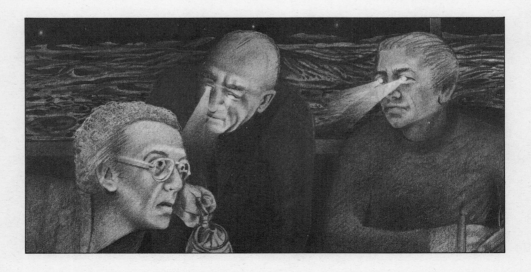

MAIN IDEA

4. Look at the ideas below. Check the ones you think are important points the story makes.

_____ Never misjudge the intelligence of your enemy.

_____ Things aren't always what they seem to be.

_____ Don't assume that what is familiar is "superior."

_____ What seems good to you may not seem good to someone else.

_____ People should be made to do what you think is right.

_____ People who have power are always right.

_____ People from different backgrounds have different customs which ought to be respected.

_____ Even the most careful plans don't always work out as expected.

_____ People should do what they are told, even if they disagree.

_____ It's never right to rebel against authority.

DETAILS

5. Heidel had _____ bullets in his gun.

SEQUENCE

6. The Council members knew that Martians could see in the dark _____.
   a. after Heidel shot out the last candle
   b. when they were babies
   c. after hearing of Dr. Kingly's experiment

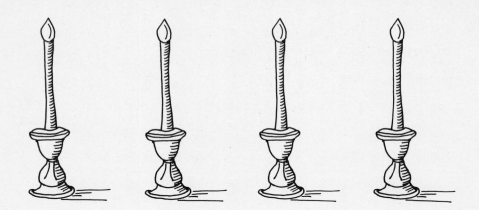

FINDING PROOF

7. Martians were smart. Proof of this is _____

_____ .

8. The butler was a Martian. Proof of this is _____

_____ .

CAUSE AND EFFECT

9. Heidel suspected that someone on the Council was a spy because

_____ .

MAKING INFERENCES

10. Why did the five Martian Council members pretend they were from

Earth? _____

_____

11. When the Council members heard Heidel's plan to shoot out the candles and catch the traitor, they felt _____.
    a. guilty
    b. safe
    c. afraid

WHAT DO YOU THINK?

Why did the Martians reject the things Earth people tried to give them? Do you think they were right or wrong? Why?

When Heidel said, "This is where we take the clothes off the sheep and find the wolf," what did he mean? From his point of view, who was the "wolf"? Who might the Council members have considered to be the wolf?

Why didn't the members of the Council kill Heidel during the years he was President? Why did they let him stay on as President? Do you think people can be happy in a country that is taken over by another country? If so, under what conditions?

WHAT'S THE STORY?

Every story has a **plot**. A plot is the "what happens?" of a story — its action or story line. Every plot has six parts. Sometimes, one part is stronger than the others. Sometimes, parts run into each other. It may be hard to tell where one part ends and another begins. But it takes all six parts to make a story.

"The Eyes Have It" is an example of a story with a strong plot. The events of the story are arranged in a cause-effect pattern. One event leads to another, which leads to another, and so on. Each event is an important link leading to the outcome of the story.

Read about each part below.

Part 1: **The introduction.** We find out the setting: Mars. We learn who the characters are: members of the Superior Council of the occupied planet. We find out where they came from: Earth, not Mars.

Part 2: **Crisis.** Every story develops around a problem or conflict that must be solved. In "The Eyes Have It" the crisis is: Who is the imposter? Which member of the Council is really a Martian?

Part 3: **Rising Action.** We learn why the imposter is a problem — and what Heidel plans to do to find him and destroy him.

Part 4: **Climax.** Heidel shoots out the candles and finds out that all the Council members are Martians. This event is the turning point in the action of the story. This is the high point of the story — the part with the greatest dramatic tension.

Part 5: **Falling action.** It is brief in this story. There are just a few details that lead to the end of the story. Heidel says he still has one bullet left. He's told that it won't do any good to fire it, for the Martians have him covered.

Part 6: **Resolution.** At the story's end, we learn how the opening crisis is resolved or settled. Heidel is in the hands of the Martians. And he finds out, as a final bitter twist, that even the butler is a Martian.

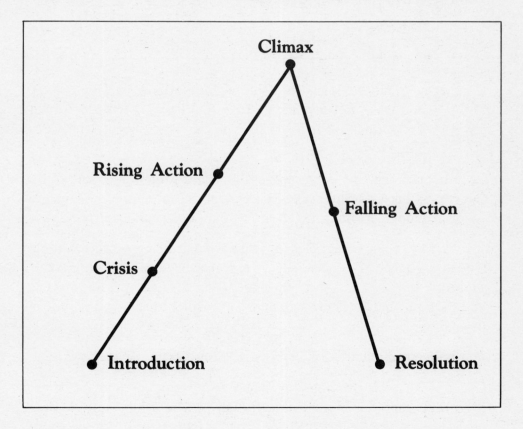

The diagram above shows the six parts of a plot in order. Start with the point at the lower left, move up to the climax, then down to the resolution to trace the pattern of a story.

Below is a story, but its paragraphs are scrambled. Put the paragraphs in order so they make sense and fit the diagram. Write the number of each part of the plot next to the correct dot on the triangle on page 141.

1. "All right," said the man. He held the cat out to the officer. "No!" Mrs. Sims cried. "Not my Jeepy! Take him home, Mister. He's better off with you than at the pound. You can have him if you'll take good care of him."

2. "Mister, stealing cats is a crime in this state," the officer said. "Besides, he's her cat. She loved him enough to do what's best for him — even though it broke her heart. Come along with me now."

3. "No!" Mrs. Sims cried so loudly that a policeman crossed the street. "What's going on?" he asked. "That man has my cat," Mrs. Sims sobbed. "It's my cat," the man said. "Well, I guess I'll have to take him to the pound," the officer said, "if neither of you can prove you own him."

4. The policeman lifted Jeepy into Mrs. Sims arms.

5. One day she left the door open and Jeepy ran out into the street. Mrs. Sims ran after him. She saw a tall man in a blue suit pick him up. "Mister, that's my cat!" she cried. "No, lady," the man said, "he's mine. His name is Fletch."

6. Mrs. Sims had a cat named Jeepy. She loved him very dearly.

THE MASCOT

Who was the mysterious mascot who cheered the team into winning the championship? Who was inside that crazy half-bear, half-bird costume?

VOCABULARY STUDY

cheerleader — someone who cheers a team to victory
mascot — person, animal, or thing thought to bring luck
enthusiasm — great interest in something
fuse — cord that can be lit to set off an explosion
cartwheels — turning sideways on the hands
pyramid — figure made up of three-sided shapes
theory — idea not yet proved
bellowed — roared; shouted very loudly

Fill in the blanks in the story below with words from the list above.

Zeb Zims loved life and met every day with _____.
He liked to go out on his lawn and turn _____ on his
hands, while his lucky _____, a black cat, ran beside
him. He had a _____ that it was healthy to sit inside a
tent shaped like a _____, and did so every day. On the
Fourth of July he loved to set off firecrackers, lighting the
_____ of each one and then jumping up and down on
the grass, waving his arms like a _____. But he did
not like his neighbor, Mrs. Zooch.

One sunny day he took his razor and mirror out in the yard to shave.
Mrs. Zooch was passing and said, "Oh, Mr. Zims, you're shaving outside."

"Of course I am," Zeb _____. "Did you think I was...?"

(Turn the book upside down to find out what Zeb said.)

FUR LINED

THE MASCOT by Megan Stine and H. William Stine

"It's just a slight slump, boys," Coach Millard told his basketball team in the locker room at half-time. But what looked like a slight slump to Coach Millard looked more like a 10-year losing streak to everyone else at Buxley High School.

The cheerleaders still came to the games, but only because it was a nice, quiet place to do their homework. Sometimes they outnumbered the fans.

"You know what this team needs?" said Harper Johnson, one of the players.

"Some good basketball players wouldn't hurt," said Mickey Linder.

"We need to do something about our spirit," Harper said.

Then Coach Millard gave one of those pep talks for which he was known all over the state. "Boys," Coach Millard said, "What more can I say?" Then he left the locker room.

Suddenly Harper picked Mickey up by the shoulders and shook him, saying, "You heard the coach. We need spirit! Now we're going out there and we're going to play like we've never played before!"

They did go out there and they did play like they'd never played before. Within minutes they were behind 79–21. And that's when they saw — IT.

All of a sudden, it was just *there* — almost as if it had fallen from the sky. The fans stopped watching the game, and the players started running into each other because no one could believe what he saw. Some guy in the craziest animal costume was running back and forth on the basketball court.

"Look at the mascot," someone from the other team yelled.

But no one from Buxley could explain it. They'd never had a mascot before.

The mascot was covered from head to foot in brown fur, including his hands and funny animal head. The head had green feathers, but it resembled a bear's head.

Every time Buxley got the ball or made a basket, the mascot started cheering in the strangest voice anyone ever heard.

"Tell the security patrol to throw that guy out," Coach Millard bellowed.

But Harper Johnson's eyes started to light up. "Coach, leave him alone! Don't you see? That guy's cheering for us. He thinks we can win!"

And soon the crowd began to pick up the funny mascot's enthusiasm. They began to imitate his funny noises, screaming every time Buxley got the ball.

Buxley won the game, 95 – 90. And that crazy mascot, whoever it was, lit a fuse under the whole school.

"Who could it be?" everyone wondered.

More people came to the next game just to see if *he'd* be there. Just as before, when no one was looking, he appeared out of nowhere. He screeched, he ran, he did cartwheels and backflips. And the team caught fire, beating Parker High 88 – 62.

As the season wore on, the crowds grew larger and louder. Brown fur hats with green feathers began popping up everywhere in the crowd. The team kept winning, but they still didn't know who their new mascot was because he always got away. Somehow, after every game, the funny costume disappeared.

Everyone had his own theory about who the mascot was. It was all people talked about in school and all over town. Everyone had theories, but no one had proof. That's why Harper Johnson felt so good about figuring it out. Harper had narrowed it down to two people, and he knew it had to be one of them.

"Who are they?" Harper's older brother, Bo, asked. Bo was leaning into the engine of his new car.

"Well, it could be Loonie Louie. He's the biggest class clown."

"You're right," Bo said, "except

for one thing. I saw Loonie Louie in the bleachers last night, while you were playing the game.''

''Well, then that leaves just one person,'' Harper said.

''Hand me the wrench, will you? Who do you think it is?'' Bo finally asked.

''You!''

Bo stuck his head out from under the hood. ''You've got to be kidding,'' he said.

''It's the only thing that makes sense. I could kick myself for taking so long to think of it. You love that basketball team. You played on it for four years. And even though the team never won a game, you played your heart out each week. You even slugged me once for saying something bad about Coach Millard.''

The two brothers stood looking at each other for a while.

''You're crazy,'' Bo said.

''You don't have to tell me if you don't want to, but I know. And I think you're terrific for doing it,'' Harper said.

''Hand me that screwdriver. I think you've got a screw loose,'' Bo said.

Mickey picked Harper up before the big championship game. They were both nervous, but neither one wanted to admit it.

''You ready?'' Mickey said.

''As ready as I'll ever be,'' Harper

said. He turned to his brother. "Bo," he said. "You *are* coming aren't you?"

Bo was eating a chicken leg and drinking a glass of milk.

"He'll be there — for sure," Harper said. "Stoke up. You're going to need a lot of energy tonight." Harper gave his brother a wink.

Bo shrugged and went back into the kitchen.

The Claymore High team played like a steel machine that night. And Buxley just couldn't get started — mostly because their minds were somewhere else. "Where is he?" they asked each other. "Why isn't he here?" Coach Millard asked during a time out.

"Don't you see?" Harper said. "He doesn't *have* to be here tonight. He showed us that we can win if we want to. We've got it inside us to win!"

Unfortunately, Harper was wrong — absolutely wrong. They played as badly as they used to. One half of the huge gymnasium was silent, while the other half yelled with glee.

Suddenly, the Buxley band was on its feet. They were playing the fight song to beat the band. The crowd leaned forward as a spotlight swept the gym and stopped at a doorway. For a moment, no one could be sure what was going on. Then a high-pitched screech rang out in the gym and announced that the mascot was there!

Probably stayed at home for another chicken leg, Harper thought to himself.

All at once, Claymore started to lose the game. Buxley blocked Claymore's shots and made impossible shots of their own. And every time Buxley did something great, the mascot did something greater. He did leaps and jumps he had never tried before. He carried a pyramid of Buxley cheerleaders. He led the crowd in cheers until everyone's throat was sore. He even ran over and hugged Coach Millard during a time out.

It was all just too much for the Claymore team, and they fell apart in the fourth quarter. When the final buzzer rang, the place went crazy. The score was Buxley 100, Claymore 92.

"We want the creature! We want the creature!" the crowd chanted. They were determined to find out who was under the costume. The crowd blocked the door. When the mascot found one door blocked, he ran to another. Finally, with a deafening screech, the mascot pushed into the middle of the crowd and fell to the gymnasium floor.

"Bo!" Harper screamed, pushing people out of his way, and running to his brother. "Bo, are you all right?"

Harper bent down beside the mascot.

"Of course I'm all right. Why shouldn't I be?" Bo said. Harper's head jerked up and his eyes opened wide. Bo was standing behind him, looking down at the floor.

"You're not the mascot?" Harper's heart was racing. Somehow, he knew then what he hadn't known before.

"Pull off his mask," someone yelled from the crowd. Harper leaned down to tug at the furry face mask. His hand touched warm flesh.

"It's not a mask!" he gasped. The crowd gasped too.

The creature's eyes opened. They darted around wildly. Then, with incredible speed, it leaped to its feet and hurled itself through the stunned crowd. Before anyone could touch it, it had dashed to one of the unblocked doors and disappeared into the night.

READING CHECK

WORD MEANING FROM CONTEXT

1. In this story, the word *pyramid* means _____.
   a. a stone monument in Egypt
   b. people standing on each other's shoulders, each line smaller until there is only one on top
   c. a kind of business arrangement

MAIN IDEA

2. Another title for this story could be _____.
   a. My Brother, the Bear
   b. Who Was the Green-Headed Bear?
   c. The Only One Who Listened to the Coach

DETAILS

3. The mascot looked like _____

   _____.

SEQUENCE

4. The mascot first appeared on the court _____.
   a. before a game
   b. after Buxley High was behind 79 – 21
   c. just as Harper made a basket

CAUSE AND EFFECT

5. People began wearing brown fur hats with green feathers because

_____.

FINDING PROOF

6. Loonie Louie was not the mascot. Proof of this is _____

_____.

MAKING INFERENCES

7. The mascot was really a _____

_____.

WHAT DO YOU THINK?

Could this story really have happened? Did you have any idea how the story might end? If so, what gave you the idea? Do you think a mascot like this one could really make that much difference in team spirit? Was it the mascot, or something else? What?

Who — or what — do you think the mascot really was? Do you think the people of the town ever really found out? If so, how?

FACT OR FICTION?

Some stories you read are true-to-life. They could really happen. Other stories are *larger*-than-life. These stories would not really happen in everyday life. "The Mascot" is one such story. What other ghost story, science fiction story, or fantasy have you read that fits this category?

On the next page are plot summaries of stories you've read. Read each one. Then check the column that best describes each story.

	True-To-Life	Larger-Than-Life
A girl pretends that she has a soldier boyfriend.	——	——
A boy gets stuck in time and lives the same day over and over again.	——	——
A man has a conversation with a picture of his uncle.	——	——
A boy saves a teacher from a burning building.	——	——
The walls of a room shrink and trap a girl who has come to paint them.	——	——
A boy gets into a fake "time machine" and comes out with a dinosaur egg from the distant past.	——	——
A young man outsmarts a crooked car dealer.	——	——
A plain girl thinks she has been tricked by a popular boy, then realizes that she was wrong.	——	——
A boy is greatly affected by the death of a classmate.	——	——

WRAP-UP

"The Mascot" ends when the creature runs out of the gym. Who is the mysterious creature? And where did it come from?

In not more than 10 sentences, write a new ending to the story. Here are some ideas that may help to get you started. But if you have a better ending, use it!

Bo follows the creature and sees a flying saucer circling overhead. He...

The coach gets home and finds an empty fur suit and a green feathered hat on his steps. A note, written in green ink, is attached. It says...

When the football season comes, the football coach gets a strange phone call. The voice is...

That night, Harper hears scratching on his bedroom door. He...

One of the team members spends a day in the woods. He finds a large nest with bits of fur and green feathers in it. He...

The high school catches fire one night. People see "something" coming to the rescue and putting out the flames. They see that...

_____

_____

_____

_____

_____

_____

VOCABULARY REVIEW

Here are some words you have learned in this book. Write them where they belong in the nonsense story that follows.

accompanied   conquered   intent   sauntered
ancient   disgrace   intimidated   scowled
bellowed   disturbed   leash   shrieked
canines   foolishness   plunge   threatening

In _____ times, fierce and cruel Norse sailors _____ many lands. They _____ the people in those countries with their meanness. The Norse Vikings _____ proudly through the streets, _____ by large _____ with sharp teeth.

One day, some brave people threw a _____ around a big Viking's neck. Some people _____ things like "dumb ox" at the man. Others made _____ gestures. "You are a _____!" they all cried as they led him to a river bank.

At the river, the leader of the people _____, "Do you know what we're going to do with you? We're going to _____ you into this river and drown you! Then we'll skin you and make a fur coat out of you!"

The Viking _____, but he did not seem _____. "Your _____ is silly. It is pure _____," he said. "Everyone knows that ... *you can lead a Norse to water, but you can't make him mink.*"

END-OF-BOOK ACTIVITY

Story Outline

An outline is a useful way to organize your thoughts and opinions about a story. On page 160 is a list of activities that you will have a chance to do. Read the list and decide on your activity. Then turn back to this page and complete the outline. You won't have to fill in every line — just those you need for your activity.

Outline For: _____

(title)

_____

(author)

A. Main characters

1. _____

2. _____

3. _____

B. Time and setting of story

1. _____

2. _____

C. Summary of plot (main conflicts, how they were resolved, climax)

1. _____

_____

_____

D. Theme or "message" of the story (the point the author wants to make)

1. _____

2. _____

3. _____

E. What makes this story stand out from others of its kind

1. _____

_____

F. Your opinion of the story (supported by details from the story)

1. _____

a. _____

b. _____

2. _____

a. _____

b. _____

You've r————————————————————————book and others.
For this rev———————————————————————ies you've read.
Select one a———————————————————————u do it, complete
the outline ———————————————————————ed.

- You are a ——————————————————————l." Select a story
  that stand———————————————————————ons for its being
  nominated ———————————————————————

- Write a le———————————————————————you've read. Tell
  a little ab———————————————————————d should read it.

- Write a diary entry covering an important scene from a story you've read.
  Write the diary entry as the main character would have written it.

- Describe an experience you've had that is similar to an experience of
  a character from one of the stories. Compare the experiences, pointing
  out the similarities and differences.